The Misunderstanding
of the Church

The Misunderstanding
of the Church

Emil Brunner

Translated by Harold Knight

The Lutterworth Press
Cambridge

Published by
The Lutterworth Press
P.O. Box 60
Cambridge
CB1 2NT
England

e-mail: **publishing@lutterworth.com**
website: **http://www.lutterworth.com**

ISBN 0 7188 9134 1 hardback
ISBN 0 7188 9133 3 paperback

British Library Cataloguing in Publication Data:
A catalogue record is available from the British Library.

First published 1952, reprinted 2002

Copyright ©1952 Emil Brunner

PREFACE

WHAT is the Church? This question poses the unsolved problem of Protestantism. From the days of the Reformation to our own time, it has never been clear how the Church, in the sense of spiritual life and faith—the fellowship of Jesus Christ—is related to the institutions conventionally called churches. This problem has become sharper than ever as a result of the ecumenical movement; but it is in no way solved and the idea of the reunion of the churches—understood by many "ecumenicals" to be the real goal of the movement—shows as nothing else how inadequately the depth of the problem has been appreciated.

For the Roman Catholic church this problem does not appear to exist at all. Rome presents to the world the face of a church which is certain of itself. But this is only so in appearance; in reality Rome too has no ready answer to the question how the phenomenon visible in the New Testament as the *Ecclesia* is to be related to the papal church as the latter has developed in the course of centuries; and the uneasiness of those who cannot satisfy themselves with the neat formula that the one has evolved into the other is the less easily appeased the longer it lasts. In the last 50 or 100 years New Testament research has unremittingly and successfully addressed itself to the task of elucidating for us what was known as the *Ecclesia* in primitive Christianity—so very different from what is to-day called the Church both in the Roman and Protestant camps. It is, however, a well-known fact that dogmatists and Church leaders often pay but small attention to the results of New Testament research, and are only too ready to bridge the gulf between then and now by a handy formula such as that of development, or by appealing to the distinction between the visible and invisible Church, and thus to give a false solution to this grave and distressing problem. But while many theologians and Church leaders are able to quieten their consciences by such formulae, others are

5

so much the more painfully aware of the disparity between the Christian fellowship of the apostolic age and our own "churches", and cannot escape the impression that there may perhaps be something wrong with what we now call the Church.

In the present work an attempt is made to discover the ground of this disharmony by systematically turning to account the conclusions of New Testament research in their bearing upon the problem of the Church as it confronts us to-day. The title of the book, *The Misunderstanding of the Church*, is equivocal. Is it a question of a misunderstanding of which the Church is guilty or of a misunderstanding of which it is the victim? Or is it that the Church itself, as such, is perhaps the product of a misunderstanding? The author is not responsible for this ambiguity; it is intrinsic, rather, to the theme itself.

It is in fact the opinion of the author that the Church itself, in so far as it identifies itself with the *Ecclesia* of the New Testament, rests upon a misunderstanding. Therefore he must be prepared for violent opposition from all those who are resolved to defend their own church as the true Church at any cost. Since for his part he does not intend to pit his views as a dogmatic system against that of any particular church, he would like to have his work understood as a contribution to the ecumenical discussion, in the course of which he is sincerely anxious to learn from disagreement. On the other hand he hopes to gain the concurrence of all those to whom Jesus Christ is dearer than their own church, and he counts with certainty upon the interest of all who wish to investigate deeply the problem of the Church. For this book has sprung from just this desire to discover the reason why since the Reformation epoch a real solution to the problem of the Church has not been found. The reader will feel, I hope, that behind it lies not merely the impulse to know, but a desire, at least equally strong, to bring into being the true fellowship of Christ.

Zürich, Easter, 1951.

CONTENTS

Chapter One

THE SUPERNATURAL CHRISTIAN COMMUNITY AND
THE PROBLEM OF THE CHURCH

IN his classical work—*Institutio Christianae Religionis*—which has probably exercised a greater influence than any other writing upon the theology of Protestant Christianity, Calvin does not begin his teaching concerning the Church until the last and fourth book, that is, not until he has in his third book discussed the dogma of justification by faith. This order of treatment, which has subsequently been adhered to by all reformed theology, is not self-explanatory nor is it lacking in significance. It is both an expression and a cause of that Protestant individualism which is so often deplored. Certainly Calvin decisively repudiates the crass individualism which interprets the Church merely as a sum of individual believers, and he appropriates the expressions of the most ancient Church Fathers to the effect that the Church is *"omnium piorum mater"* (1) and *"extra ecclesiam"* is *"nulla salus"* (2).

These phrases, however, suffice at most to conceal, but not to overcome, the fundamentally individualistic outlook which determines Calvin's conception of the Church; for in reality, and in the last analysis, Calvin means by the Church simply the *ecclesia invisibilis*. The visible Church, on the contrary, is relegated by him to the dubious category of *externum subsidium fidei*, of an "external means of salvation" (3). Now the idea of the invisible Church is foreign to the New Testament, while the interpretation of the real visible Church as a merely external means of salvation is not only foreign to it but completely impossible. Never did it occur to an apostle that the *Ecclesia*, the fellowship of Christian believers, the true people of God of the New Covenant, might be regarded simply as

9

a means to an end, and even at that a purely "outward" means.

Such an understanding of the Church seems to all catholic-minded thinkers a horrible blasphemous heresy, and therefore they are compelled to condemn as such Protestantism as a whole. Must we not say that they are right from the standpoint of the New Testament? Perhaps both parties, Catholics —and I do not mean primarily *Roman* Catholics—and Protestants are right and wrong at the same time. Certainly— from the point of view of the New Testament, of what is there called *"Ecclesia"* and of what the *Ecclesia* understands itself to be—the thought of Calvin, that the Church is an external support for faith, is utterly unintelligible. The New Testament *Ecclesia* realizes that it is the Body of Jesus Christ, that it is divine revelation and salvation in action, therefore never to be thought of as a means to an end, but as an end in itself, even if as yet only an adumbration of a yearning for the consummation which shall be in God's good time. But the thought of Calvin which within this context seems unintelligible becomes immediately all too plain as soon as we translate *"Ecclesia"* by "Church", and in so doing think of the institution with all its paraphernalia without which the historical Church is simply inconceivable. The Catholics are right: the *Ecclesia* of the New Testament is no *externum subsidium fidei*, but the real thing. The Protestants are right: what the Church has become as a matter of historical fact is not the real thing, but something which may very fittingly be understood as a means to an end.

The *Ecclesia* of the New Testament, the fellowship of Christian believers, is precisely *not* that which every "church" is at least in part—an institution, a something. The Body of Christ is nothing other than a fellowship of persons. It is "the fellowship of Jesus Christ"[1] or "fellowship of the Holy Ghost",[2] where fellowship or *koinonia* signifies a common participation, a togetherness, a community life. The faithful are bound to each other through their common sharing in Christ and in the Holy Ghost, but that which they have in common is pre-

---

[1] 1 Cor. 1:9.   [2] 2 Cor. 13:13; Phil. 2:1.

cisely no "thing", no "it", but a "he", Christ and His Holy Spirit. It is just in this that resides the miraculous, the unique, the once-for-all nature of the Church: that as the Body of Christ it has nothing to do with an organization and has nothing of the character of the institutional about it. This is precisely what it has in mind when it describes itself as the Body of Christ.

At the beginning of the history of the *Ecclesia* stands the mystery of Pentecost. When Christianity classifies the feast of Pentecost with the other great feasts, with Christmas, Good Friday and Easter, each of which reminds us of one of the solemn mysteries in the story of our redemption—the Incarnation, the Atonement, and the Resurrection—it wishes to teach us thereby that the outpouring of the Holy Ghost likewise (and that means the rise of the *Ecclesia*) is one, and, in fact, the last of the great saving miracles in the process of revelation. The outpouring of the Holy Ghost and the existence of the *Ecclesia* are so closely connected that they may be actually identified. Where the Holy Ghost is, there is the Christian communion. And the Holy Ghost is not otherwise there than as the Spirit given to the community. Therefore the community as bearer of the Word and Spirit of Christ precedes the individual believer. One does not first believe and then join the fellowship: but one becomes a believer just because one shares in the gift vouchsafed to the fellowship.

It is idle to ask which comes first, the egg or the hen, for both points of view are true. But the question whether the word of Christ or faith comes first admits of no discussion, for faith is the response to the word of Christ. This word is entrusted to the keeping of the Christian fellowship, not, however, as an abstraction, but as the Word of the living Christ, who abides in the fellowship through the Spirit. Therefore the fellowship of Jesus precedes the individual believer as the *mater omnium piorum*. Only by taking this insight seriously can we transcend both Protestant individualism and Catholic collectivism. For the Church is neither a *numerus electorum*, a totality of believers, nor is it a sacred institution, but it is the Body of Christ, consisting of nothing but persons:

of Him who is the Head and of those who are members of His Body.

The *Ecclesia* is what it is through the presence of Christ dwelling within it. He is present with it through His Word and His Spirit—"the Spirit of truth which shall lead you into all truth".[1] Therefore, because the Holy Spirit is the very life-breath of the Church, the Church participates in the special character of the holy, the numinous, the supernatural, in the hallowing presence of God: for that reason the Christian society itself is a miracle. It is therefore in point of fact unintelligible from a purely sociological standpoint (K. L. Schmidt).[2] For it is in fact intelligible only from the standpoint of the Christ who dwells within it and determines its life. And so because it is itself the "temple of the Holy Spirit"[3] it is in its very essence the sphere of the holy and needs no temple. The fact that it is both *koinonia Christou* or *koinonia pneumatos* and "fellowship one with another",[4] thus combining the vertical with the horizontal, divine with human communion (4)—that fact constitutes its entirely characteristic, its utterly unparalleled life.

The togetherness of Christian men is thus not secondary or contingent: it is integral to their life just as is their abiding in Christ (5). But this fellowship of the society does not exist independently and in its own right: it flows from communion with Christ. For this reason we may see how impossible it is to describe the Church as a means to a higher end. The fellowship of Christians is just as much an end in itself as is their fellowship with Christ. This quite unique meeting of the horizontal and the vertical is the consequence and the type of that communion which the Father has with the Son "before the world was";[5] in the supernatural life of the Christian communion is completed the revelation of the triune God, and the Church has therefore done right to order the celebration of the Holy Trinity on the Sunday after Pentecost. For the very being of God is *Agape*—that love which the Son brings to mankind from the Father, and it is just this

[1] John 16:13. [2] See note 5. [3] 1 Cor. 3:16; 6:19.
[4] 1 John 1:7. [5] John 17:5, 24.

love which is the essence of the fellowship of those who belong to the *Ecclesia*. Hence this love is called the "bond of perfectness" of the *Ecclesia*.[1]

In the *Ecclesia* lies the answer (though of course even there it is tainted with the imperfection which clings to everything human) to the two fundamental questions with which humanity is confronted, the question of truth and the question of human fellowship. Here we see *the* truth which is a fellowship and *the* right relation of men with one another arising from the fact that their life is rooted in the truth. The truth is the love revealed in the Son as the image of the Father and the ground of all that is: and this very love is the being of that society which was founded by Jesus Christ and whose life is continuously inspired by Him. By this shall men know that its members are His disciples. One dwells in this love through faith, and through faith one participates in the fellowship. But a man cannot acquire this faith except in so far as through love he inheres in the fellowship. Truth and fellowship are here one and the same thing.

God has not revealed abstract neutral truth or truths, a dogma or dogmas, supposedly committed to the keeping of the Church as a *depositum fidei*, as something which the latter *credendum proponit* (6): but God has revealed *Himself* in Jesus Christ in the personal presence of Immanuel, of the Word made flesh. The *fact* that God has revealed Himself and *what* He has revealed are therefore one and the same thing: namely, the truth that His very nature consists in His communicating of Himself in love, in His self-donation for man, in His *Agape*. Thus one cannot enter into His self-revelation merely by believing in a dogma, but only inasmuch as one has communion with Him through the Son, and therewith ceases to be an isolated individual. In so far as one learns to know God, who gives Himself for us and wills to dwell with us, in so far as one learns to know Him in such wise that to know Him and to dwell with Him are one and the same, one is brought into the life of self-impartation for, and communion with, mankind. Fellowship with Christ and fellow-

[1] Col. 3:14.

ship with men are correlative, the one cannot exist without the other.

Communion with God which is not also communion with man is a false attitude—all such a-social mysticism is wrong: equally false however is a communion with mankind which is not also and primarily a communion with God—that is to say, all irreligious or godless communism is wrong. Jesus Christ is the Truth and as such He founds a communion of God and man which puts an end to all isolation. Therefore Christian truth can be apprehended only in the Christian fellowship. The *Ecclesia*, the Christian society, thus itself belongs to the substance of the revelation and constitutes the true end of the latter. Walking in the light of the revealed truth and walking in the fellowship which that truth has brought into being are inseparably bound up. Consequently it is impossible to consider communion with the *Ecclesia* as a means to an end; it must be realized that it is the end itself, though in its earthly form; this final goal of the *Ecclesia* is still imperfectly attained.

We may conclude that the thought of the Church as a mere means of salvation would never have occurred to Calvin, had he not read into the idea of the New Testament *Ecclesia* the image of the institutional Church as it has historically developed. In this, however, he does not stand alone: Catholics before and after him and Protestants of all shades of opinion contemporaneous with him have done likewise. What divides them is simply this, that from this erroneous identification they have drawn different conclusions. Because the *Ecclesia* of the New Testament is an end in itself and not a means to an end, the Church is an end in itself and not a means to an end—say the Catholics. Because the Church is an external institution and not the movement of salvation itself, it cannot be an end in itself but only a means to an end—so say the Protestants: but both parties err in that they understand the *Ecclesia* of the New Testament to be the historical Church. The latter is rather something which has arisen, in the course of a long and complicated history, through a process of development, transformation and retrogression, out of the New

Testament *Ecclesia*. That in view of these various historical manifestations which go by the name of "church", one may, indeed must, arrive at the conclusion that the Church is only a means to an end, a means of salvation, but not the reality of salvation itself—all that is not only understandable but correct. Hence arises, however, the difficult problem of the Church, which resides in the ambiguous relationship between the New Testament *Ecclesia* and the institutional church known to history. For of this church—whichever of its historical forms we may be considering—it cannot be said that it is a pure communion of persons. Much rather is it of the essence of this entity, the Church, that it is not only "church" but a thing, an institution.

Of all the great teachers of Christianity, Martin Luther perceived most clearly the difference between the *Ecclesia* of the New Testament and the institutional church, and reacted most sharply against the *quid pro quo* which would identify them. Therefore he refused to tolerate the mere word "church": he called it an "obscure ambiguous" term (7). In his translation of the Bible, he rendered the New Testament "*Ecclesia*" by "congregation", and in his catechetical writings he paraphrased the credo ecclesiam with "Christendom" or Christian Community (8). He realized that the New Testament *Ecclesia* is just not an "it", a "thing", an "institution", but rather a unity of persons, a people, a communion, and as he had a thorough knowledge of his New Testament he knew and emphasized that in it the *Ecclesia* is often spoken of where the actual word is not used: the equivalent expressions, however, are always of a personal nature: the Israel of God, the seed of Abraham, the elect priestly race, the people for God's own possession, etc. The word *Ecclesia* itself, however, means congregation, people of God (9).

Strong as was Luther's aversion to the word "church", the facts of history proved stronger. The linguistic usage of both the Reformation and post-Reformation era had to come to terms with the so powerfully developed idea of the Church, and consequently all the confusion dependent upon the use of this "obscure ambiguous" word penetrated Reformation theology. It was impossible to put the clock back by one millenium and a half. The conception "church" remained irrevocably moulded by this historical process of 1,500 years, as a result of which the *"Ecclesia"*—a communion of persons—had been transformed into an institutional "church", and indeed into that particular church in which the momentum of institutional development had reached its climax, that church which interprets itself in a severely institutional sense, viz. the Roman church. The whole history of the Roman church is the history, carried to its remotest consequences, of a progressive, consistent, and complete institutional distortion, or more precisely, legalistic distortion. The Roman church understands itself—since the *Vaticanum* and *Codex juris canonici* of 1918 there can be no more doubt about it—in the sense of the sacrosanct Canon Law. In the *Vaticanum* and the *Codex juris canonici,* everything which the church is, has, and gives, is brought under the heading of Canon Law; even the definition of dogma is part and parcel of the papal *potestas jurisdictionis.* Here it may be 'seen how the movement, which began at the close of the first century, has reached its ultimate term: the replacement of a communion of persons by the legal administrative institution (10).

If the church is an institution—and in some sense all who use the word "church" mean this (11)—then Rome is the most churchly church, the norm of ecclesiastical life; for in her the institutional distortion of the *Ecclesia* is completed, and in her alone. If by the word "church" one means something other than Rome (12) then one must be sure to analyse radically this different conception: then one may not translate *"Ecclesia"* by "church", nor may one desire to set up a "church" in the Name of Jesus. One must then recognize that the *Ecclesia* of the New Testament, the Christian fellowship of the first Christians, was not a "church" and had no intention of being a "church".

The example of the Roman church—the fully churchly "church"—shows us negatively what the New Testament exhibits positively. The *Ecclesia* as *koinonia Christou* and *koi-*

nonia pneumatos, as the Body of Christ, is a pure communion of persons entirely without institutional character.

Since Augustine (13) but especially since the time of Zwingli and Calvin, with the growing realization of the discrepancy between the New Testament *Ecclesia* and the historical "church", quite useless attempts have been made to elucidate the relationship between the two quantities by drawing a distinction between a visible and an invisible church. This expedient is of no avail simply because the invisible church is not a fellowship but a *numerus electorum*, hence a fundamentally individualistic conception: but no more is the visible church a fellowship; it is rather an institution, a collective, hence an external, means of help. Both the one and the other fail to tally with what was intended and realized in the New Testament: the communion of the fellowship with Christ which as such meant also the communion of the members one with another.

For centuries now in the sphere of Protestant theology this desperate expedient has been vainly used in the attempt to explain the disparity between the actual churchly institution and the New Testament idea of the *Ecclesia*. But these twin conceptions, so far from clarifying what was intended, have served but to increase the confusion. The insistence upon identifying the specific historical reality called the "church" with the *Ecclesia* of the New Testament has effectively prevented a solution, while the fatal idea of the invisible church has perforce served to make impossible a true insight into the nature of the problem.

This insight—which an unprejudiced study of the New Testament and the crying need of the church have helped us to reach—may be expressed as follows: the New Testament *Ecclesia*, the fellowship of Jesus Christ, is a pure communion of persons and has nothing of the character of an institution about it: it is therefore misleading to identify any single one of the historically developed churches, which are all marked by an institutional character, with the true Christian communion. Not until this view has been explored from every angle may one proceed to the second question: in what relation do these various historical institutions called "churches" stand to the *Ecclesia*, the fellowship of Christ, and in the light of this norm, what is their value and their mission? The consideration of this problem will determine the course of our inquiry.

Chapter Two

THE HISTORICAL ORIGIN OF THE "ECCLESIA"

(a) *God's people in the Old and the New Covenant*

IT is easily forgotten that the primitive Christian Community began its existence as a Jewish sect (1). It was some considerable time before the first church in Jerusalem freed itself from the cultic obligations of Judaism in which, of course, all the apostles had been nurtured. Their first place of assembly was naturally the temple, in whose life the earliest Christians continued to participate without much sense of inconsistency. We know how deeply they were agitated by the question as to how far the Jewish ritual and food laws and prohibitions, and, above all, the requirements of circumcision, still possessed validity for them. Only gradually and after violent struggles was a final release from Judaism attained and did it become recognized in consequence that the Christian society was utterly distinct from and indeed irreconcilable with the Jewish church. Not only in this early period, however, but throughout the whole course of Christian history up to the present time, it has proved impossible to answer with a plain "Yes" or "No" the question whether or not the fellowship of Jesus Christ is something new in contradistinction to the people of God according to the Old Covenant. Such a question can only be answered with a "Yes" that must be at the same time a "No", and a "No" that must also be a "Yes". This dialectical relationship is not the result of a confused insight, but springs from the essence of the matter in question.

The *Ecclesia* of Jesus Christ is God's people, the elect people —that was also the rightful description of Israel. For the conviction of election, arising not from their own patriotic over-estimation, but from the revealed word of the prophets, had been from the beginning the inspiration of Israel's religious consciousness. Israel is the covenant-people of the covenant-God—that, however, is precisely what the *Ecclesia* of the New Testament apprehends itself to be. It would seem, therefore, that according to the purpose of God the *Ecclesia* was to be identified with the elect people of the Old Covenant. And yet the fellowship founded by Jesus realized that it was something wholly new, namely, the fellowship of those who through Jesus Christ share in the New Covenant and the new aeon. Although the church since Irenaeus (2) has been accustomed to explain this relationship of identity and non-identity as due to the difference between two different economies or dispensations within the course of one and the same stream of redeeming history, this explanation cannot be made quite to correspond either with the first Christians' own interpretations of their community, or with the historical facts. On the contrary, Jeremiah had already raised the expectation of a "new covenant" which "would not be as the old covenant which God had concluded with their fathers"[1] and the *Ecclesia* itself is aware that through the present fulfilment of what had been previously merely promised, not simply a new *modus dispensationis* but an utterly new dimension of salvation has been vouchsafed, namely, life in the Holy Spirit, concerning which the Gospel of St. John roundly declares "for the Holy Spirit was not yet given".[2] When Paul affirms: "If any man is in Christ he is a new creature"[3] he is alluding to a new mode of existence not yet known to the believers of the old covenant.

This new mode of existence in the new covenant, therefore, characterizing the life of the *Ecclesia* in contradistinction to that of the Old Testament people of God is especially recognizable in three facts. Firstly, the ceremonial and cultic laws of Israel and Judaism are no longer valid for the *Ecclesia*. This issue was especially at stake in the struggle which Paul had to fight out with the exponents of the doctrine of continuity: for those who belong to Christ, circumcision is no longer a valid requirement.[4] To assert the continued obligation of circumcision would be nothing less than to disown and lose one's

[1] Jer. 31:31ff.   [2] John 7:39.   [3] 2 Cor. 5:17.   [4] Gal. 5:6.

relationship to Christ. At this point the particularism of a Jewish sect was transcended and superseded by the universality of the new humanity—in Christ. This meant a break with the Temple cultus due to the recognition that Jesus Christ Himself has offered the only perfect sacrifice, consequently is the only true high priest, and that this His sacrifice has been offered once for all.[1] With this recognition, the idea of a distinction between priesthood and laity has forever ceased to be tenable.

In all this was implied, secondly, a clear discrimination between membership of a nation or race and membership of a community of believers. This distinction is now explicit: for already within the framework of the Old Testament itself such a distinction is at least implicit—that between the true Israel, the true people of God, and the Israel to whom God addressed His relentless "Not my people".[2] Even within the Old Testament itself it is already a question of a "Remnant" springing up within the physically constituted Nation. This Remnant, however, was never separated off. But such a separation was now effected through baptism in the name of Christ, whilst that other distinction—the wall of partition[3]—between born Jews and born Catholics—was at the same time abolished; the Gentiles who are in Christ are quite as fully citizens of the new heavenly *polis* as are those of the circumcision.

A third conclusion was implied, namely, that the civil laws of the Old Testament prescribed for Israel as a national, political entity were no longer relevant. From the point of view of constitutional law, the *Ecclesia* stands under the jurisdiction of the Roman Emperor and Roman jurisprudence, and this heathen order was granted complete recognition as the divinely appointed one,[4] in spite of the fact that it stood in no sort of historical continuity with the process of special revelation. As far as secular politics are concerned, the *Ecclesia* is no longer subordinate to the Jewish theocracy, but to the avowedly secular government of the Roman state. *Ipso facto* the *Ecclesia* renounces every kind of theocratic pretensions;

---

[1] That is the theme of the Epistle to the Hebrews.
[2] Hosea 1:6; 2:1.   [3] Eph. 2:14.   [4] Rom. 13:1-5.

theocracy, the fusion of Christ's rule with the law of the state, is henceforth given up, just as much as the Temple priesthood, and the laws of the Sabbath and of circumcision, are given up.

Therein resides the otherness of the new dispensation as compared with the old: but its otherness cannot be fully grasped by such a comparison; it consists above all in the new dimension of life in the Holy Spirit and the new aeon, which Jesus Christ has not merely announced, but also inaugurated. Therefore there now ensues the plain and unambiguous outward secession from Judaism to which there corresponds inwardly the self-description of the *Ecclesia* as the true Israel,[1] the Israel of God[2] in opposition to the description of Judaism which rejects Christ as the "Israel after the flesh":[3] this secession, however, does not imply the renunciation of the hope of an ultimate reunion through the conversion of the Jews to Christ.[4]

(b) *Jesus and the Ecclesia*

The approach to an understanding of the relationship between Jesus and the *Ecclesia* has been obstructed by the translation of the term *Ecclesia* without more ado by the term "church", as a result of which the question has been formulated whether Jesus founded or instituted the church, and further because it has been too little realized that there are appointed stages in the process of saving history, that God travels with men along a road of which the end and the beginning are far apart. Revelation is progressive; to the present phase of the process there corresponds a specific mode of existence of the *Ecclesia*. If we bear in mind these two considerations, the question whether the only two places[5] in which Jesus speaks of the *Ecclesia* are genuine or not will appear somewhat beside the point. Whether with the older school of critical scholarship we deny this genuineness or whether with the more recent and no less critical school we affirm it, two points in any event remain indisputable: Jesus

---

[1] John 1:47; Rom. 9:6.   [2] Gal. 6:16.   [3] 1 Cor. 10:18.
[4] Rom. 11:23ff.   [5] Matt. 16:18; 18:17.

did not "found" the Church; and Jesus unquestionably gathered around Himself a circle of disciples of such as were specially related to Him and whom He specially equipped and sent out in His service.

When we recollect how long the Church took to become clear about its relationship with Judaism, we must not expect Jesus—who never forestalled historical developments, but was content to fulfil His appointed task in history—to have expounded any kind of doctrine about the *Ecclesia* and its relationship to Judaism and the Temple. His mission in the process of redemption and revelation was not to announce the coming of the Messiah, but to be the Messiah, and to be, in particular, the veiled, the "incognito" Messiah. The veil does not begin to be lifted until His death upon the Cross draws near: in the same degree His teaching concerning the character and function of discipleship becomes clearer (3).

From the very beginning, however, He had chosen disciples whose existence may be counted as among the firm constituents of the tradition. The twelve are from the start a fixed feature of it, whose certainty not even Paul ever doubted, although he may well have been sorely tempted to do so. If Jesus knew Himself to be the secret Messiah He could not help doing precisely what tradition reports Him to have done: He gathered around Himself a body of His own, to whom "it is given to understand the mysteries of the Kingdom of God" in contrast to "them that are without".[1] But He collected this circle around Himself in such wise that in it too the "incognito" was preserved. A visible separation from the Jewish community could as little be thought of as Jesus' own self-revelation as the Messiah: both events could, of course, only have been misunderstood. But everything speaks for the reliability of the tradition according to which the Last Supper was the occasion when the Master, in sight of His approaching end, revealed to His own their true significance as the community of the New Covenant (4). Up to that point His band of disciples remains the secret following of the secret King.

[1] Mark 4:11.

With the first Easter all that changed, and the change was openly exhibited in the event of Pentecost.

The community which had been founded and fashioned anew through the events of the passion, death and resurrection, at Pentecost stepped forth out of its concealment; the Messianic secret is now disclosed and at the same time the interpretation of the Messiahship of Jesus transformed; He is now hailed as Messiah—a Messiah who is also the vicariously suffering Servant of God, the Lord who is present with His own through His Spirit. Henceforth the body of disciples are moulded through the "fellowship of the Spirit". They live not by the inspiration of a historical memory; but He with whom they had eaten and drunk is now in the midst of them.[1] He, the Lord, present through the Spirit, is the life-principle of the *Ecclesia*. But since the Spirit is the present gift of salvation, He is also the earnest (*aparché*)[2] of that which is to come. As the communion rejoicing in the here-and-now presence of the Saviour, the *Ecclesia* at the same time yearns for the future consummation with tense expectancy. And precisely that gift which is present miraculous possession—the Holy Ghost—is the link which as a pledge (*arrabon*)[3] united her with the coming, future One.

So finally the question whether Jesus "founded the *Ecclesia*" is seen to be of small moment: the *Ecclesia* is in any event rooted in Him and interpenetrated by Him, since He is the head of the body which is the *Ecclesia*. The gift of the Holy Ghost and the sharing in the invisible presence of the Master are so closely connected that it is hardly possible to distinguish between them, but rather it may be said: "The Lord is the Spirit."[4] So then the fellowship of Jesus is the true people of the covenant, whose history doubtless begins with the old covenant, but which only attains full reality through the living presence of the Risen Lord. But because the fellowship is nothing else than this people of God dwelling in the Spirit, it is in no sense an institution, but the living body of the living head.

---

[1] Matt. 18:20; cf. below, p. 64. [2] Rom. 8:23.
[3] Eph. 1:14; 2 Cor. 1:22. [4] 2 Cor. 3:17.

Chapter Three

THE APOSTLES AND THE FELLOWSHIP

Our interpretation of the Christian community will be decisively orientated by our interpretation of the apostolate and its significance for the *Ecclesia*. Here especially the ways of the Catholic and Protestant churches diverge. If we are to arrive at an agreed definition of the *Ecclesia*, it is at this point, therefore, that we must concentrate our investigation. First of all, we must take as our point of departure the incontestable witness of the New Testament itself that the *Ecclesia* is built upon the foundation of apostles and prophets.[1] What does that mean? In what sense is the authority of the apostolate or of the apostolic office to be understood?

The fellowship of Jesus Christ is the work and product of His word and spirit. It is rooted in the historical unrepeatable fact of revelation, in the Word made flesh. By that is meant that it is rooted in a contingent fact, here and not there, happening just then and not at any other time; hence in a saving event which is determined in space and time, in the life, passion, death and resurrection of Jesus Christ. The Gospel is thus no timeless truth, but truth which has been enacted on the plane of history[2] and which as such must be reported and announced. So the Gospel is dependent upon the report of eyewitnesses, upon the preaching of those who were with Him. "Ye shall be my witnesses"[3]—that is the fundamental commission of the Risen Lord to His ambassadors, His apostles. This office of bearing witness at first hand is therefore that which constitutes the apostolate (1).

Upon this witness depends the whole future of the Christian communion. What they have received they must pass on to the world. And what they have received has the full weight

[1] Eph. 2:20.   [2] John 1:17.   [3] Acts 1:8.

25

of ultimate divine authority. Without the apostles there would be no Christianity: or, more exactly, without the divine authority of the apostles there would be no *Ecclesia*. The fellowship of Jesus is only conceivable, only operative, as an apostolic fellowship.

Is that not the thesis of the catholic church? Yes, certainly, and not only of the Roman, but of all catholic churches. What is more, it is the thesis of the Reformed churches. Not the thesis as such divides us, but its interpretation. It must, of course, be admitted that in the more modern types of Protestantism a false interpretation of the thesis has brought about a rejection of the thesis itself. In contradistinction to modern rationalistic expositions, which equate the universal priesthood of believers with democratic conceptions, we must first emphasize with the catholics: in the *Ecclesia* of the New Testament period the quite undemocratic and hierarchical position of authority occupied by the apostles is grounded in the fact that they alone are the primal witnesses of the saving history, that all others must receive the word of salvation from them alone and from them alone can it be received. To clash at this point is to clash not with catholic but with Christian foundations. The contingency of the revelation in history conditions the contingency of the pre-eminence assigned to the apostles.

This consideration, of course, qualifies in two ways the nature of the apostles' divine authority. This authority is, in the nature of the case, untransferable. Much can be handed over to others, but one thing can never be: namely, the authority of one's personal presence at an event, the authority of an eyewitness, the standing in the first link of the historical chain. And it is just this kind of testimony which constitutes the authority of an apostle. In face of the great fact of special revelation, no other kind of inequality can subsist but this— that some receive it at first hand as eyewitnesses, while all others must receive it through them, if they are to have it at all. The peculiar pre-eminence of the apostles, grounded solely in the contingence of the historical fact, is therefore absolutely limited by this cause. Their authoritative position is

26

likewise contingent, as unrepeatable as the revelation itself; it is therefore in the most strict and unqualified sense, untransferable. In other words, it is transitory: it vanishes with the physical existence of the eyewitnesses. This very transitoriness is likewise implied in the fact of revelation as such. It cannot be otherwise: it can, of course, be understood in another sense, the transitory can be made permanent, the untransferable can be transferred, but when that happens, it happens *per nefas*, as the result of a radical misunderstanding.

The authority of the apostles is in yet another sense transitory, not merely in the sense that it passes *away*, but also in the sense that it passes *on*. The sole source of the authority of the apostles lies, of course, in what they have received: therefore, for the reason that they alone have it, all others are dependent on them. The authority resides wholly in the gift itself, in the contents of which they are the vessels. Therefore it is inevitable that when this gift is conveyed to others, the latter share now in what the former originally held exclusively. Authority is imparted to the receiving community in proportion as the apostles effectually convey what they have to convey. Time may be needed before this process of transfusion from the primary to the secondary vessels is completed, and as long as the process lasts, so long lasts also the authority of the donors; but once the gift is really given, once the Word of Christ has really been conveyed to the community, appropriated and as it were absorbed by it, then indeed the community has— what is alone the source of authority—the Word of God (2). Only in one sense there remains a relation of dependence on the apostles' words: the form of the fundamental apostolic word is still valid as the criterion by which each Christian community must test its own existing word in order to make sure that the two are identical.

With the extinction of the physical existence of the apostles one thing is bequeathed by them, which will be useful and indeed necessary as a norm and critical touchstone of everything which claims authority in the community, namely, their written word. This will come up for discussion later. The apostles, whose authority lies solely in the divine gift given to them that they may impart it to others, must themselves endeavour to diminish their own authority more and more in order that the community may be made ever more independent by the completest possible appropriation of the saving gift, the word of revelation. The more "of age" the community becomes, the more can the apostles reckon with it as equals;[1] only its minority, the incompleteness in its assimilation of the proffered salvation, makes it to all appearance lastingly dependent on the apostles. This immaturity, however, is not a necessary but a fortuitous thing, something which must disappear, can disappear and does in fact finally disappear.

Such is the character of the apostolic authority as becomes apparent from our insight into the nature of the revelation itself; no other character *can* be assigned to it except through a misunderstanding. But after we have thus grasped the meaning and the limits of apostolic authority through, as it were, deductive reasoning from the intrinsic nature of the saving revelation, we feel it necessary to test this result by the data of the New Testament itself. To be sure, it soon becomes obvious that our theory is not expressed so perspicuously and unambiguously in the pages of the New Testament as we could wish. On the contrary, there are in the New Testament not inconsiderable traces of quite another conception and estimate of the apostolic office, and this is just the reason why people so often talk at cross purposes. We find side by side in it not only the interpretation of the apostolate which we have just outlined, but also quite other theories largely in conflict with it; firstly one which seems to suggest a permanently authoritarian hierarchical organization of the church and yet again, on the other hand, one which diminishes still further the authority of the apostolate (3). We must come to terms with the fact that there does not exist in the New Testament that degree of unity which orthodoxy has continually postulated and presupposed. Hence the discussion cannot be furthered simply by the production of a proof-text, for in problems of this sort it has always been possible to prove from

[1] I Cor. 3:1; cf. I Cor. 2:15, Heb. 5:12.

28

the New Testament the exact opposite of what was required. The only thing that can help us is to reflect upon the inner significance and purpose of the New Testament witness upon the conclusions which necessarily emerge from the facts themselves, and in which, as we shall see, the declarations of the New Testament documents plainly culminate.

Since the famous dissertation of Karl Holl concerning "Paul's idea of the church in comparison with that of the primitive community" (4) it has become unmistakably clear —even though one may not thoroughly agree with Holl's thesis at every point—that side by side with the Pauline conception of the *Ecclesia* and its order there existed yet others, for example that of the first Judaic Palestinian church in Jerusalem, which bore an essentially more authoritarian character. There was not only this one, however; rather we can see to-day the emergence of three theories of the primitive Christian society: (i) the Pauline; (ii) to the right, so to speak, the Palestinian-Jerusalem one; (iii) to the left, as it were, the Johannine. Whilst the second greatly emphasizes the administrative authoritarian aspect, and the third, on the contrary, relegates this to a subordinate place, even to the point of failing to give due recognition to apostolic authority, Paul holds an intermediate position between the two extremes.

In this connection the Jerusalem conception of the apostolate is of special significance. There is no doubt that it deviates seriously from that of the apostle Paul, for according to it a lawful administrative authority, so to speak, seems to have been formally granted to the first apostles, who exercised a sort of authoritarian government of the church. But in this regard the following consideration is decisive. When sharp exchanges of opinion were taking place in the so-called apostolic council concerning the question of circumcision, that is, concerning the question of the validity or otherwise of the Jewish ceremonial law, there did *not* happen what alone according to a formal juridical conception of apostolic authority should have happened, but, on the contrary, there happened what according to this conception was an utter impossibility:

the newly received apostle Paul was able through his superior spiritual and theological insights to convince the first apostles that Christian faith and the insistence upon circumcision were mutually exclusive. All along the line the new apostle's conception made itself felt and in spite of the fact that he gave way in no single point, the apostles separated from each other extending the right hand of fellowship.

All this implies nothing less than the fact that the finally decisive authority was not that of any apostle as such—a hierarchical canonical authority—but simply and solely the truth of the Christian message, the power of the living Word. This again means that besides the interpretation of the apostolate inherent in the character of the revelation, there really existed another, arising *per nefas* from a radical misunderstanding, that this other erroneous conception dissolved under the impact of the spirit-filled Word of Christ uttered by Paul, and that in the last resort Christian vision alone and no personal apostolic claim was recognized as final. One cannot, therefore, say that the second, wrong, interpretation is unknown to the New Testament; but one must add that this misconception was recognized as such and that believers confessed the sole validity of Christ's authority, as manifested in His Word and Spirit. The Word and the Spirit won a victory over nascent Canon Law. That it happened here, however, does not mean that it happened everywhere, and not, above all, that it was to happen always. On the contrary, we see that Paul was continually encountering this false claim to authority on the part of "the very chiefest apostles"[1] and had continually to overcome it through the power of the living Word and Spirit until finally beyond the boundaries of the New Testament it gained a decisive triumph. Within the New Testament epoch itself, however, we see an as yet quite inconclusive struggle not merely between these two but between three outlooks, which cohered with divergent conceptions of present and future salvation (5). But we cannot speak of a consistent development in one particular direction, that is, in the direction of later catholicism, for the reason that the most

[1] 2 Cor. 11:5; 12:11.

anti-hierarchical, the Johannine outlook of the late New Testament period is just as much an integral part of it as is the outlook of the Pastoral Epistles, which is moving in the opposite direction: in that of hierarchical catholicism. That is why in this matter nothing can be decided by merely quoting "proof texts", but rather it is necessary to reflect upon the essential nature of the thing itself, of the fact of salvation in Jesus Christ, in order to find the real and true New Testament conception.

In conclusion it remains for us to deal with an argument which is advanced by Catholics not without considerable cogency. It may be formulated thus: the whole thesis so far expounded—"a typically Protestant one"—overlooks one decisive factor. It takes into consideration only the authority of the *word* of Christ, not however that of the *will* of Christ and its ordering, unifying function in the church (6).

Jesus Christ sent out His apostles as His personal plenipotentiaries and equipped them not only with the authority of the Word, but also with personal authority by their direction to give shape and coherence to the growing church. This might be described as apostolic authority in the stricter personal· sense. It finds expression again in the fact that the apostles on their part sent out their representatives with full personal authorization to guide the church as a whole and administer its affairs. Thus there is not merely an authority of the word, which is transitory in the previously discussed sense, but also an administrative authority, not interchangeable with that of the word, dependent therefore on personal authorization and transferable. Protestantism suffers from a failure to acknowledge or appreciate this administrative or authoritative aspect of the apostolate and of the church generally (7).

What are we to say about this Catholic standpoint? Every officer knows that the efficiency of an army depends upon the clean-cut and firm power to command, upon formal competence, upon relationships of superiority and subordination. We do not fail to recognize that in every church—the more so in proportion to its greatness—a similar need exists; but we are not concerned here with the needs of a church, we are concerned to inquire what was the true state of affairs in the *Ecclesia* of primitive Christianity.

From the history of the apostolic council, of which Paul gives a standard account in the Epistle to the Galatians, we were led to see that such formal authority to command was indeed claimed in certain sections of the church, but that it was certainly not conceded by Paul and that finally it yielded to the power of the Word and Spirit of Christ. The New Testament church—as will be shown in Chapter Five—was an astonishingly well-ordered whole without such a formal hierarchy, without such delimitation of competence and regulation of rank. And not only a well-ordered but also a coherent whole. The unity of the Christian fellowship flowed from the living Word and Spirit of Christ dwelling within it. Doubtless the apostles were granted without demur a certain leading influence in all things appertaining to the common life of the communion. But again the paradoxical peculiarity is this: that they never claimed this ascendency as a formal right accruing to them through their institution as apostles, but rather in everything they strove to gain the assent of the communion and submitted themselves to the test of authentication by signs and wonders in the power of the Holy Ghost.[1] Only so was it possible that the primary apostles should give way to the new apostle Paul and then indeed not reluctantly, just for the sake of peace, but with genuine conviction and subdued as they were by the Spirit of Christ speaking through him.

Three further facts point in the same direction. The apostles were certainly equipped by Jesus with full authority as His ambassadors; at the same time nevertheless they received the strict order to go forth not as rulers but as servants, just as the Master Himself, through His readiness to serve, through His surrender to death, had become the victor over principalities and powers.[2] In this sense, precisely through its inner connection with the imminent death of the Cross, the story of the foot-washing is essentially true and historical, although it

[1] Rom. 15:19; 2 Cor. 12:12.   [2] Phil. 2:8f.; Col. 2:15.

may not be so from the point of factual information. Thus and not otherwise had Jesus interpreted and granted to His emissaries plenitude of power and authority (8). Secondly, when Paul is enumerating the various *Charismata* to which special types of service are adapted, he includes the charisma of *Kybernesis*, of government,[1] as one amongst others without according to it the slightest degree of preference. This service too is needed, so he argues, and the *charisma* corresponding to it exists; but this service is only one among others and authorizes no sort of hierarchical structure. Further, even those to whom this service is committed must continually prove themselves to be worthy and capable of it;[2] any formal right to its exercise is thus completely excluded. Such an interpretation alone harmonizes with the conception of service embodied by the Lord Himself who ruled through lowliness.

Thirdly: the apostles of the first Jerusalem church, indeed the latter itself, enjoyed special pre-eminence within the *Ecclesia* as a whole, because the preaching of the Gospel had originated with them, hence by reason of the already explained factor of historical contingence. But the recognition of this priority, as is especially clear in the case of Paul, was an entirely voluntary thing and was kept within quite definite limits. His deference towards Peter and the "pillars" did not hinder him from fighting to maintain his cause, the cause of the truth itself, in defiance of these authorities; and likewise the latter did not obstinately insist upon their primary status, but submitted to the sway of truth. But what became of the Jerusalem claim when its historical destiny overtook that city? The privilege of priority linked to this place vanishes completely. After the death of the apostles, the apostolic office retains its value in one way only: as providing the norm of the fundamental tradition now committed to writing, of the fundamental testimony, that of the New Testament. This does not mean, as is so often mistakenly assumed by Catholics, that the oral word is to be finally replaced by the written; the Christian communion still has its prophets, men filled

---

[1] 1 Cor. 12:28.   [2] 1 Cor. 16:15.

with the power of the Spirit; it has become no synagogue of mere scriptural exegesis. But the Scripture is the norm of all dogma, because it crystallizes the primary shape of the tradition and hence becomes regulative for the teaching of the church (9).

Chapter Four

THE CHRISTIAN FELLOWSHIP AND TRADITION

It is no error that many churches should ascribe the highest decisive importance to tradition; on the contrary, it is consistent with the essential nature of the Gospel. A serious recognition of tradition is integral to the Gospel itself. We must remember, however, that tradition may be understood in very different senses. In the history of the Church it is possible to distinguish between three notions of tradition, each of which has a quite distinctive content and whose connection with the original revelation varies—the primitive Christian, New Testament notion, the early catholic one, and the neo-catholic Roman one. We must consider each of these separately.

(a) *The primitive Christian notion of tradition*

Tradition is necessarily involved with the unique revelation of God in the historical facts concerning Jesus Christ. This unique historical event, in which the disclosure of salvation is contained, must be conveyed to later generations in order that they may share in its saving benefits. *Paradosis, traditio* belongs, therefore, to the very nature of the Gospel; to preach the Gospel means necessarily and always to transmit an account of what has happened for man's salvation.[1] Without tradition, no Gospel. The mere fact that the Word became flesh, that the eternal truth of God disclosed itself in the substance of history, implies that tradition is the indispensable instrument for the extension in time of the revelational happening. If this is what we mean by tradition, then from the outset there can be no fundamental antithesis between Scripture and tradition, between the oral and the written communication of what has happened in Christ and of what has been received through Him. On the contrary, when

[1] cf. *paralambanein* and *paradosis*.

35

it is a question of preserving as accurately as possible for suc-
ceeding ages some historical event, fixation in writing is the
supreme means adopted by tradition. So far as the contingent
historical fact implied in revelation is concerned, the crystallization of the tradition in writing, the primary witness of the
New Testament Canon is the standard means by which tradition operates. All later accretions must be judged by the
measure of their conformity with this fundamental testimony:
the canon is the "rule", the norm of tradition. Certainly it is
true that oral tradition preceded Scripture and also that, in
this sense, the Church preceded Scripture. The New Testament was the product of the primitive community. But such
considerations do not affect the fact that this tradition fixed
in writing must be and must remain the sole criterion of all
later oral developments. Otherwise there is no guarantee that
the same fate might not be in store for the Christian Gospel as
overtook, for example, the teaching of Zarathustra or that of
the Buddha—namely, that in the course of oral development
something utterly different was evolved out of it. Anyone who
is concerned to see that the Christian datum itself as the decisive thing should be handed down to us, the later generations, in its original purity, must assign to the written tradition this supremacy as the norm for all oral accretions, precisely in order to maintain the authenticity of the tradition
itself.

(b) *The early catholic notion of tradition*
But the Church evolving out of the fellowship of Jesus
sought to create a second, and quite different, means of guar-
anteeing the genuineness of the tradition, that is, of preserving it in its original purity: not only did it establish and define
the Canon of the New Testament as the normative fundamental testimony, it also created, as such a guarantee of
genuineness, the office of bishop continuous with that of the
apostles. The reason for the establishment of this new guarantee lies without question in the struggle which it cost the early
Church to control the rank luxuriating gnostic heresies. It
was vital to erect a dam against them, and the Church—for

36

in this period we must already so describe the fellowship of Jesus Christ—believed that the formation of the apostolic episcopate was such a safeguard. Irenaeus's theory of tradition at the close of the second century was conceived in this sense. The unbroken chain of teachers officially recognized as bishops by the community—the apostles forming its first link —constitutes the surest means of preserving the continuity of apostolic doctrine. But this means was of questionable value, and, as we shall see, showed later that it might endanger the very end for which it was created. Even supposing that the uninterrupted apostolic succession of bishops could be proved —which despite Hegesippus's lists of bishops is more than doubtful—who could guarantee that the bishops thus ordained in unbroken succession were really the bearers of the original apostolic doctrine (1)? Here there took place evidently a very understandable and obvious, but yet critical and suspicious, change in the conception of tradition. The principle of tradition as consisting in the continuity of the thing itself, of truth, was replaced by the notion that tradition consisted in continuity of succession in office or in legitimacy.

This modification in the idea of continuity was, of course, not noticed because it was in fact probable that those selected by the apostles as bearers of the Gospel message with which they were entrusted offered a better guarantee of its faithful delivery than any other persons: with each passing generation, however, this probability decreased until all security vanished. The further the Church became removed in time from its historical origin, the less likely was the continuity of mere succession in office to assure the continuity of the thing itself, of the message handed down from the apostles. Even if we suppose that all who held office in this unbroken succession were subjectively of the opinion that they taught nothing but what the apostles had taught from the very beginning, yet a comparison of the dogma of the church in the second with that of the church in the fifth or still more the eleventh centuries shows conclusively that this subjective opinion was not objectively accurate. The dogma *did* change.

The Church itself could not altogether fail to recognize this

37

fact. But it sought to justify itself both in its own eyes and in those of the world—perhaps never with complete awareness —by combining with the thought of tradition in the original sense, that is, as preserving the pristine purity of the Gospel, a second quite different conception, one which in any event is always present in notions of tradition prevalent among Catholics to-day: the thought of the unfolding of something which was originally only latent into its fully explicit and, as it were, mature form. By means of this notion it became possible to identify the new with the old, without being compelled to deny the element of newness. What is to be said about this new understanding of tradition?

Even from the standpoint of the most rigorous Biblicism there is fundamentally nothing to object to in it. On the contrary, in the New Testament itself we see at work just this process by which what is at first given only in seed blossoms into its fullest flower. Nay further: the Master Himself had promised His disciples that the Holy Spirit would lead them into all truth.[1] And the apostles also had often enough expressed to their congregations the hope and the expectation that they would grow in insight and understanding.[2] It is a completely unfounded assertion to say that this principle of development was unknown to antiquity and that it was not discovered and applied until the modern era. The ancients likewise understood the principle of natural growth; they too realized that the tree develops out of the seed, the man out of the child, and this idea of natural expansion and growth is certainly not foreign to the New Testament.

Besides, every preacher "expounding" a text makes use of this conception. His exposition presupposes that in the text lies something more or less hidden which can only be developed from an implicit to an explicit stage by the technique of exegesis or *explicatio*. That such a process actually took place within the New Testament itself in a significant manner and at critical points is to-day disputed by hardly any New Testament critic who, for example, compares the primitive Christian witness of the Jerusalem church with the theologically

[1] John 16:13. [2] Col. 1:11; Eph. 4:15.

38

mature testimonies of a Paul or a John. But why should that which went on quite justifiably in the New Testament itself not also be allowed to happen in the course of church history? We must go yet one step further and say: this process of development has in fact taken place in the evolution of church doctrine. Thus, for example, the doctrines of the Incarnation and the Trinity are, to be sure, latent in the New Testament but reached their full development and definition only through subsequent theological reflection. Therefore, it would be a very short-sighted and, even from the standpoint of the New Testament, an unjustifiable Biblicism which would disallow the notion of development out of the embryonic to the finally mature.

In any event, the early Church acted upon this principle in complete good faith and endorsed the formula of Vincent of Lerins as expressing her own belief: true apostolic doctrine is *"quod semper et ubique et ab omnibus creditum est"*. And in order to prove the identity of her present doctrine with that preached by the apostles, she made special use of the means by which the primitive Christian Church tried to demonstrate the inner connection of the Gospel with the Old Testament, namely, that of the "proof-text".

Now, however warranted this notion of development may be, it is not without its dangers. For it may happen all too easily that, with the aid of such a theory, an identification of quite another kind may take place: the equation of terms that are not equal, the equation of things that are plainly incompatible. Therefore, quite a different sort of process might easily be exchanged for that of *development*—the process of *transformation* and *distortion*. This *quid pro quo* could so much more easily arise in that the process of transformation was effected slowly, continuously, and in small, hardly perceptible stages. Even such tiny deviations can cumulate in the opposite of the original term. The continuity of this movement of deviation and its imperceptibility, thanks to the small stages by which it is accomplished, does not affect the fact that the final result may be antithetic to, and irreconcilable with, the original. And that is precisely what, side by side

39

with the process of development, actually took place in the early Church—though for the above-mentioned reason imperceptibly.

Now this fact is intimately connected with just that modification in the notion of tradition which we discussed first: with the tendency to equate unbroken succession in office or legitimacy with continuity in the sense of preserving the original deposit. The apparent continuity of the succession, the regulated sequence of ordination, in short, verifiable legitimacy, produced the appearance of a real and substantial continuity. Not only so, but when once tradition and office had been in this way made coincident, the fiction of necessity arose that in a church whose order was thus secure, continuity of essential meaning must likewise be guaranteed. Continuity in *office* seemed to make the demonstration of continuity in meaning superfluous, to the point of eliminating it altogether as a possibility. Belief in the apostolic succession of bishops seemed to offer enough security to guarantee the *semper et ubique* without any such exact positive proof. The *office* became an unproved and unprovable guarantee of truth.

Yet another logical fallacy, closely related to what has already been argued but not quite the same point, is necessary to a right understanding of the notion of tradition implied in early catholicism. It is a mistaken opinion frequently to be observed—current even within the context of modern evolutionary thought—to suppose that what changes slowly, continuously, gradually, and in accordance with principles of organic growth, does not in reality change at all, but remains essentially the same. Hence not only does the latter remain unnoticed in consequence of the gradualness of the change, but there is added to the psychological failure a logical one, namely, the confusion of two different things. Perhaps this failure in logic was less real in the early Church than in the modern renascence of early Catholic thought, for it is notorious that this renascence stood under the influence of a romanticism which made the greatest possible use of this unhappy idea of organic development (2). The same is true finally of a theory which likewise plays a noteworthy part in contemporary Catholic thought—more than in that of the early Church: a theory, to wit, which introduces the concept of Providence in the philosophy of development. God has so ordained it, at least so permitted it, hence such a development must be right. This use of the concept of Providence receives no encouragement from the Bible, but springs from a very different intellectual source; it is a mode of the Hegelian principle: "The real is the rational." It is, therefore, an evolutionary line of thought, resting upon metaphysical-religious foundations, to ascribe value to the historical process as such, and to regard it as being necessarily a channel for the continuous unfolding of truth. It goes without saying that in this way every heresy can be justified, if only it results from a steady uninterrupted process rather than from the violence of revolution. This philosophy contains in itself nothing less than the abdication of truth before the forces of history—a phenomenon which, in the era of Marxism, is neither unknown nor without its dangers.

Thus we see that in the early Catholic notion of tradition a series of completely heterogeneous elements are at work, which yet are held together through the single magic word "tradition"—tradition in the sense of preserving the purity of the original Gospel, as in primitive Christianity: tradition in the sense of legitimate ecclesiastical succession; tradition in the sense of organic development: tradition in the sense of equating development with gradual transformation: tradition in the sense of continuous historical evolution generally. What, however, in spite of everything unites early catholic with primitive Christian notions of tradition is the *bona fide* opinion that in all this it is really a question of the unanimous voice of the Church in all periods, according to the formula of Vincent of Lerins. Now that is just what separates early catholic ideas of tradition from those prevalent in neo-catholicism (3).

(c) *The neo-catholic Roman idea of tradition*

What happened in the middle of the twelfth century in the western Roman church is astonishingly little known, although it is of enormous significance. This state of affairs arises from the fact that in non-Roman Christianity the theologians for the most part do not know enough about jurisprudence, while the lawyers do not understand enough theology in order to grasp and measure the full import of what then took place in the Roman Curia.

Until then, matters stood thus—that "canon law was in the hands of the theologians" (4); the essence of early Catholic canon law is expressed in the maxim that "its knowledge is not juridical but theological knowledge" (5).

For canon law up to that point is defined as "the law appertaining to the sacraments of the church" (6). Church government and administrative power flow from the privileges conferred by the sacrament of ordination (7). What takes place now in that period?

Two things. First, lawyers schooled in the science of Roman law enter the Curia. They think in the categories of Roman law, of the *corpus juris civilis*. And this shows itself secondly in that they introduce for the self-determination of the Church a notion which had been unknown to the early Church but which from henceforth is to shape the whole life and thought of the Church: the notion of the Church as a corporation. The Church ceases to be Christianity represented in the persons of the bishops, and becomes a corporate body ruled by the Pope. From now on, "canon law is *made* by the bearers of ecclesiastical authority" (8) just as secular law is made by those who wield the power of the state. The Pope becomes a lawgiver in that he receives the *potestas jurisdictionis*. "The Church of God is administered after the manner of the state." "It engenders its law in virtue of its corporate organs." (9) "In neo-catholicism a new (legal) person has stepped in between Christ and Christianity—the Church as a corporation. . . . The Church of Christ ruled by Christ is no longer Christianity, but the Church only as a corporate institution. . . . Christ bears sway in His Christendom only through the means of the Church, that is, the churchly organization." (10) New Catholic canon law is fundamentally a body of *laws*, valid through the power and authority of the corporation from which they emanate, without regard to the *consensus ecclesiae.* "The infallibility of the Church as Christianity is changed into the infallibility of the Church as a corporation." (11) Authoritarian definition of dogma results from ecclesiastical lawgiving.

It took six centuries for this new self-interpretation on the part of the Church to become fully expressed in all its logical consequences and to succeed in establishing itself. The most important stages in the process are: the Tridentine Council when the *sine scripto traditiones* were placed on the same level of importance as Holy Scripture itself and therewith Scripture—the testimony of the apostles—not only completed by a new source of knowledge, but effectively eliminated as a final court of appeal; the Vatican Council in which tradition exactly like Scripture was eliminated in favour of the final authority of the Pope to decide matters of dogma. "What Scripture teaches, is shown by tradition—so runs the Tridentine decree: what tradition is, the church teaches—so wills the Vatican." (Loofs) (12) The last step in this direction is taken by the completed *Codex juris canonici* of 1918 in which all matters connected with the Church, both faith and morals, are subordinated to the authority of the Pope, and dogma as a whole becomes part of the papal *potestas jurisdictionis.* The Pope is no longer bound to what has always been the rule in the life of the Church; he can make new departures. He is no longer bound to the *consensus* of the Church; rather it is explicitly stated that *ex sese,* on his own authority, *non autem ex consensu ecclesiae* (13), without needing to have regard to a council, or the assembled body of bishops, he may create dogma, in virtue of his unlimited absolute *potestas jurisdictionis* which extends over the whole field of faith and morals.

Naturally the Church had to present this new state of affairs in such a way as to appear once again to combine the new with the old. For this purpose she used a means which was a sheer inspiration of genius. Scripture and tradition had to be preserved as normative factors and at the same time room had to be made for the unrestricted *potestas jurisdictionis* assigned to the Pope. The two things were made compatible by the explanation that the Pope was the sole authoritative exponent of Scripture and the sole authoritative source and interpreter of tradition. Henceforth tradition is no more what hitherto everyone understood it to be: an extant chain of witnesses binding the present uninterruptedly with the remotest past. Now tradition is instead something of which the Pope alone has knowledge and which he handles with sovereign authority. "The present has power over the past." (14) It is now *de jure* exactly as Pope Pius IX declared: "*La traditione son io.*" I, the Pope, am tradition. What the Pope declares to be tradition, that *is* tradition and every Catholic Christian must profess his belief that it is tradition, even though no trace of such a tradition exists. The absence of evidence of tradition in the customary sense can offer no difficulty: for the Pope alone has authoritative insight into what constitutes tradition. What he explains to be traditional must be believed as such, on pain of the loss of eternal felicity.

That means then: the process which began with the institution of the episcopate as the guarantee of original apostolic truth has here reached its logical conclusion. The formal institution has triumphed over living tradition. The institution as such guarantees apostolic truth. The notion of tradition has been completely emptied of its true content. Tradition has ceased to be the chain of witnesses reaching back to the original revelation; instead, it has become a myth. It is now a dormant reserve fund of the Church, from which, from time to time, the inadequate Biblical evidence is completed, a reserve fund which the Pope alone has at his sovereign disposal and in the exploitation of which no one may call him to account. Since the Council of Trent every appeal to Scripture is rendered null and void by the conception of the tradition which completes—and eventually, in point of fact, eliminates—Scripture. Since the Vatican Council every appeal to real tradition also is made inefficacious through the theory that the Pope alone has authoritative knowledge of tradition. The Pope has not only the right but also the sacred canonical duty of repudiating and disallowing every critical further inquiry based upon an appeal to Scripture or tradition and of excommunicating anyone who persists in such an attitude. Not only Scripture but tradition also is eliminated by the boundless absolute *potestas jurisdictionis* of the highest ecclesiastical office (15). The ecclesiastical office alone guarantees the compatibility of what is now accepted as valid with the original apostolic doctrine.

From these considerations it may be seen how hopeless it is for Protestants, non-Roman and Roman Catholics to discuss the rights and the wrongs of tradition, since all three mean by tradition something quite different. It may sound paradoxical but it is the fact that Reformed theology entertains the strictest notion of tradition—a notion which is identical with that of primitive Christianity. *The Reformers are the real traditionalists*; they take most seriously the idea of tradition as the preservation of the original Gospel. The laxest notion of tradition is that characteristic of Roman Catholics; by their system of canon law and ecclesiastical jurisdiction they reject the idea of any need to test received authoritative doctrine by the touchstone of apostolic teaching. No one is warranted in applying this test except he who is least fitted to do so, the official representative or rather creator of the now accepted doctrine. Between these two parties stand the "old" catholic churches with their impure notion of tradition. Since they—and in this they diverge from Roman Catholicism—have not yet formulated the dogma of the sole right of the ecclesiastical office to give a decisive interpretation of Scripture and tradition in such a way as to preclude all critical testing of received doctrine by genuine tradition and of genuine tradition by Scripture, it is yet possible to institute discussions between them and Protestants. Nay more: since they acknowledge the principle of Scripture just as much as do Protestants the idea of development, mutual understanding between them is always possible over a wide area. In such negotiations the Protestants will particularly stress the principle of Scripture, Catholics that of development, but neither will do so exclusively. Both these parties believe in the norm of Scripture and in the idea of development; but they can both only deny what the Roman Catholic understands by tradition. For here tradition is no longer the plain testimony of history, but has resolved itself into the Pope's power to annul the witness of the past.

Chapter Five

THE CHRISTIAN FELLOWSHIP AND THE HOLY SPIRIT

Behind the conception of tradition as it lives in the minds of many people to-day there lies, concealed for the most part rather than expressed, perhaps even unconscious rather than conscious, a concern for the idea (which the New Testament can only sanction) that it is not merely a question of the continuity of the word—the maintenance of the original doctrine—but also of the continuity of a life; that is, life flowing from the Holy Ghost. The fellowship of Jesus lives under the inspiration of the Holy Spirit; that is the secret of its life, of its communion and of its power. To use a blunt modern word, the Spirit supplies the "dynamism" of the *Ecclesia*. Word and Spirit are certainly very closely connected; and yet in these pneumatic energies there is something which eludes expression in words, something in relation to which all words are inadequate, if not in fact quite misleading. There exists even in the New Testament a certain tension between Word and Spirit. "The kingdom of God is not in word, but in power."[1] The apostle Paul freely admits that he won the Corinthians not through words of wisdom, but through demonstrations of the Spirit and of power.[2]

Here is indicated a reality which can reveal itself apart from words, like that power of the Spirit which struck down Ananias and Sapphira and killed them as though it had been a powerful electric current. Precisely because it is operative and yet not comprehensible in words, or rather, because the words in which we seek to grasp its nature allow the living reality to evade them and in any event do not transmit its power, expressions are used to denote it, even in the New Testament, which do not spring from the realm of logos-knowledge but from that of nature, and in particular the

[1] 1 Cor. 4:20. [2] 1 Cor. 2:4.

47

notion of power (1). Where this power exists, things happen —things which are described as mysterious, perhaps "occult", and which a generation to whom all this has become alien through excessive rationalism dismisses with the derisive term "magical". We are afraid, and not unreasonably, of this whole kingdom of the para-logical: we know, of course, that from it flow such phenomena as hysteria, mass psychology and psychopathy. On the other hand modern psychology has made us realize that these forces do not lose their efficacy by being repressed in the unconscious, but become only the more dangerously powerful. In any event we ought to face the New Testament witness with sufficient candour to admit that in this "pneuma", which the *Ecclesia* was conscious of possessing, there lie forces of an extra-rational kind which are mostly lacking among us Christians of to-day.[1]

The psychology of the unconscious serves us well in drawing our attention to the fact that, in regard to the dynamism of human life, it is precisely this layer of the soul—only too often withdrawn from clear awareness—which is the decisive factor. Now the Holy Ghost is certainly not to be identified with the unconscious. The Holy Ghost is God: but the *Ecclesia*, in its experience of the Holy Spirit, experienced God as the One whose impact on human life penetrates these depths of the soul, touches these hidden energies, mobilizes and harnesses them in the service of His holy will (2). The Holy Ghost seizes the heart, not merely the *nous*: it pierces the heart until it reaches the depths of the unconscious and even the very physical constituents of personality. Theology is not the instrument best adapted to elucidate just *this* aspect of pneumatic manifestations. For theo-*logy* has to do with the Logos and therefore is only qualified to deal with matters which are in some way logical, not with the dynamic in its a-logical characteristics. Therefore the Holy Ghost has always been more or less the stepchild of theology and the dynamism of the Spirit a bugbear for theologians; on the other hand, theology through its unconscious intellectualism has often proved a significant restrictive influence, stifling the opera-

---

[1] See note 5.

tions of the Holy Ghost, or at least their full creative manifestation. But we shall never rightly understand the essential
being of the New Testament *Ecclesia* if we do not take fully
into account these paralogical revelations of the Spirit.

If we search the New Testament documents themselves in
order to discover some characteristic signs of its mode of
being and operating, we shall have to affirm for example that
the "pneuma" is there, manifesting its presence and operating in a self-authenticating manner—even so it is said of Jesus
that He preached with authority and not as the scribes;[1] its
effects are incomprehensible, striking the beholders with
amazement and awe. The Spirit operates with overwhelming,
revolutionary, transforming results. It manifests itself in such
a way as to leave one wondering why and how, and in such
a way as to demolish the walls of partition separating individuals from each other. Its mode of operation is such that
we find ourselves forced to adopt the terminology of mysticism
on the one hand, of magic on the other, since that of logic and
even of theology is seen to be inadequate and inappropriate.
In this connection three phenomena in particular fall to be
considered, standing obviously in closest relation with the
work of the Spirit.

(i) Flowing from the revelation of the Holy Ghost was the
mysterious power which made the fellowship, consisting of
many separate individuals, into a unity, a single "body". We
must not rationalize this concept of the body—often used, of
course, in theological writing—by reducing it to a mere
metaphor. Certainly a body in the sense of a physical organism was not meant. But what was intended thereby was an
effective reality of a supra-logical kind, quasi-physical, and
in any event essentially organic (3).

This concept must not be understood either too theologically or too untheologically. It is a question—so much is
indisputable—of the body of *Christ*, therefore of a spiritual
organism which is not independent of the word and the historical fact of Christ; again, however, this must not be understood to mean a reality existing merely in theological-Chris-

[1] Mark 1:22.

tological concepts, but rather existing at least after the fashion of the living physical body—not for example (a further rationalization) a reality in the sense of a juristic corporation, or in the sense of an organization. Just as the word "dynamic" is indispensable for the characterization of the "pneuma" and expresses one aspect of its meaning most accurately, so the concept body, organism, expresses another aspect. With this is directly connected the second phenomenon.

(ii) As the differentiation of individual organs is essential to the healthy functioning of a body—there is no body without members—so to the body of the *Ecclesia* belongs its membership. This organism too had a living structure capable of functioning.[1] There was in the *Ecclesia* a regulation of the functions—Scripture declares this explicitly[2]—assigned by the Holy Ghost to the various individual members who were thus equipped to perform their special services—falsely represented as "offices". For an office belongs to a public organization; an office is part of an institution. The *diakoniai*, however, the "services", should be conceived on the analogy of the organs with their specific functions which inhere in a living body. Even though it be only a metaphor,[3] this is relatively the most adequate expression of the truth.

The New Testament surprises us again and again by the multiplicity of these functions and their bearers, of the various services and those who render them. One thing is supremely important: that *all* minister, and that nowhere is to be perceived a separation or even merely a distinction made between those who do and those who do not minister, between the active and the passive members of the body, between those who give and those who receive. There exists in the *Ecclesia* a universal duty and right of service, a universal readiness to serve and at the same time the greatest possible differentiation of functions. The metaphor of the organism illuminates one aspect of the reality; the dependence of all kinds of ministration on the one Lord[4] reveals the other. The head of a body is something different from the ruler of a people. Yet both sides of the reality are expressed and must

---

[1] I Cor. 12.   [2] I Cor. 12:11.   [3] See note 3.   [4] I Cor. 12:5.

obviously be expressed, in order to do justice at one and the same time to the vertical and the horizontal relationship, on the one hand to bring out the mysterious vital fellowship, on the other hand to show that it is the one Spirit who effects the differentiation of functions.

It is therefore quite wrongheaded to describe this pneumatic ordering of the *Ecclesia* as anarchical (4) simply because it is something different from an organization or institution. This can only be said by one upon whose mind the later juridical administration of the Church has left such an indelible imprint that he can imagine no other sort of order except that. But it is the mystery of the *Ecclesia* as the fellowship of the Spirit that it has an articulate living order without being legally organized. When we who are so accustomed to the juridical organization of the Church ask how such a "pneumatic" order is possible, the answer must be: it *is* no longer a simple possibility, but it *was* once possible thanks to the reality of whose dynamic power we can now entertain scarcely a vague surmise (5)—the reality of the Holy Ghost. From this point of view it would have to be said: The organization of the church and in particular its legal administration is a compensatory measure which it becomes necessary to adopt in times and places where the plenitude of the Spirit is lacking. Canon law is a substitute for the Spirit.

(iii) How did the fellowship of Jesus spread? We children of an era that is rationalized through and through always think first and perhaps exclusively in such a matter of what we should call evangelization, or missionary work, in which the stress lies almost wholly upon the proclamation of the Gospel, and this proclamation again is understood in the sense of theological instruction. Of course, teaching and in the broader sense preaching played a decisive part in the spread of the movement. But something at least as important was just that other, that "pneumatic" factor, the non-theological, the purely dynamic. Outsiders were attracted—the story of Pentecost already shows us this quite plainly—not primarily by what was said, but by the element of mystery— what happened simply. The impression made by the life of believers plays a part of decisive importance in the genesis of faith. People draw near to the Christian community because they are irresistibly attracted by its supernatural power. They would like to share in this new dimension of life and power, they enter the zone in which the Spirit operates before they have heard a word about what lies behind it as its ultimate transcendent-immanent cause. There is a sort of fascination which is exercised mostly without any reference to the Word, comparable rather to the attractive force of a magnet or the spread of an infectious disease. Without knowing how it happened, one is already a carrier of the infection.

Certainly, where it is a question of the *Holy* Spirit, it is also necessarily a question of the historical fact of Jesus Christ and the Word of God, for the "pneuma" shows itself to be the Spirit of God in that it testifies to Jesus Christ as the truth and the Son of God. That, however, does not mean that the Holy Spirit cannot for the most part operate without the Word, by the dynamic energy which is proper to it. The propagation of Christianity takes place to a large extent more unconsciously than consciously, more involuntarily than voluntarily, and therefore silently rather than by speech. As certainly as the explicit word and clear recognition are required for the decisive act of faith and conversion, so the obscure beginnings of faith may be, and often are, much less dependent than we theologians are inclined to admit upon the word of the preacher. Here the mighty energies of the Spirit are more important than any word, although these energies, in so far as they are those of the Holy Spirit, owe their origin to the Word of God. Present-day evangelists and missionaries usually realize this fact far better than we theologians who not only undervalue the dynamic power of the Holy Ghost, but often know simply nothing of it. With them the not unreasonable fear of an excess of enthusiasm, of the para-logical, has certainly had the effect of causing the apostle's injunction "Quench not the Spirit"[1] to be disregarded and of confining attention to his warnings against the overvaluation of this para-logical, dynamic element.

[1] I Thess. 5:19.

The Word of God is truly and effectively in the Church as the word of the Holy Ghost, implying therefore a unity of "logos" and dynamic energy which lies beyond all comprehension. From this unity, which later ceased to exist or to be understood, flows the hidden life of the primitive community. It forms the secret both of the fellowship and of its moral power; for upon the inspiration of the Holy Ghost rests the *Koinonia*, the communion of men with each other, the fact that they are knit together in an organism which includes both equality and difference, the fundamental equality of all and their mutual subordination each to other. The significant mark and the essential being of this communion consists in the quality of *agape*—the new ethos of the fellowship and its members. It is understandable that a later time, when this original power and unity no longer existed in the same abundance, should seek to find a substitute for what was lacking and to secure the presence of what was fast disappearing. This attempt at security and replacement assumes three different forms: the living Word of God is secured—and at the same time replaced—by theology and dogma; the fellowship is secured—and replaced—by the institution; faith, which proves its reality by love, is secured—and replaced—by a creed and a moral code.

It is so much easier to discuss from an intellectual and theological standpoint the ideas implied in the revealed Word of God and to analyse them conceptually than it is to allow oneself to be transformed at the centre of one's life by the action of the Holy Ghost: and further, theological ideas can be handled and arranged as one desires at any time—not so the Word of God.

It is so much easier to secure the life of the fellowship, its coherence and its indispensable hierarchy by means of solid legal forms, by organization and offices, than it is to allow the life of communion to be continually poured out upon one, to allow oneself to be rooted in it by the action of the Holy Ghost. You can handle and shape as you please such things as law and organization, but you cannot act thus towards the Holy Ghost.

And finally: it is so much easier to assent to a creed, a dogma, a firm body of teaching than it is to believe in such a way that belief is inseparable from love. Above all: one can mould as one will creeds and moral codes, handle them, teach them, learn them, but one cannot thus control that faith which is active in love.

The order intrinsic to the fellowship springing from the Holy Spirit was *diakonia*—service—the same therefore as flowed from true faith and revealed itself in a new relationship to one's brother. But the organized hierarchy presupposing the office had neither the character of brotherly communion nor had it a unity wherein equality was consistent with differentiation—a unity characterized by reciprocal subordination. The delicate structure of the fellowship founded by Jesus, and anchored in the Holy Spirit, could not be replaced by an institutional organization without the whole character of the *Ecclesia* being fundamentally changed: the fellowship of Jesus Christ *became* the church. The apparent similarity between the official organization and the New Testament order of the Spirit shows upon closer inspection that at every point there has taken place a change in essential character. The paradoxical unity of things which everywhere else exist in disparity was no longer present as the decisive factor. Now there was dogma—without the dynamism of the Spirit-filled Word of God. Now there was faith, in the sense of correct, orthodox belief, but separated from love. Now there was a community in the sense of a Church with offices, but no longer the solidarity of reciprocal service. How this, for the most part, scarcely perceptible change came about must be considered in the following chapters.

Chapter Six

THE CHRISTIAN COMMUNITY IN ITS MESSIANIC
ESCHATOLOGICAL CHARACTER

The fellowship of Jesus discloses a paradoxical unity of terms which elsewhere are incompatible. It is a mystical unity of visible earthly persons with an unseen, heavenly, and yet present Person, their Head, with the eternal ever-present Christ. One is accustomed therefore to describe the idea of the *Ecclesia* as a mystical one and to speak of a mystical approach to the life of faith (1). One may do this, only one should be aware at the same time that this mysticism is fundamentally different from all other mysticism in that it is rooted in history. For this invisible Christ, the Lord, is in fact no other than He whom the pillars of this society—the apostles—had known in the flesh as the rabbi Jesus of Nazareth, with whom they had eaten and walked in bodily fellowship, who had been amongst them in His physical presence on the last evening of His life and who on the day following had been crucified. And His death upon the cross was a very real and tangible fact of history—crucified under Pontius Pilate, for so in credal confessions this fact had been formulated in terms of world-history. It was not something which now lay forever behind them as though it had been revoked by the subsequent fact of the resurrection: much rather the fact of His having been crucified was the saving fact itself upon which all their faith was founded. Only in the unity of the Cross and the Resurrection was the life of faith possible as a being crucified with Christ and at the same time a sharing in His triumphant life (2). And not until they had risen with Him in their hearts did they apprehend within themselves His so-called mystical presence. An odd sort of mysticism this, which lives entirely in the life of a historical, never-to-be-repeated occurrence and is actually identical with this occurrence![1]

Again, this consciousness of union with the Christ, especially in what are traditionally called the sacraments, has been described as magical (3). One may so call it as long as one is also aware that this real communion with Him in His death and in His risen life was also an act of faith in what God was saying to them through this His *verbum visibile*: namely, that here was the revelation of His righteousness and love, of His justifying grace, by the effect of which they, poor sinners, are no longer sinners in His sight, but rather His dear children or sons to whom He promises the gift of His own eternal life. An odd sort of magic this, which is so completely one with faith in God's revealing Word and saving act. Of course, the fact remains that the vocabularies of both mysticism and magic must be laid under contribution in order to convey what the Christians possessed in a new life of personal communion, which far transcended all rational conceptions of human society and in a new experience of supernatural powers and gifts which lay beyond the boundaries of the sober, rational everyday world. We may go further and say that the paradoxical character of the Church has yet another decisive aspect, in virtue of which whosoever seeks to grasp this new phenomenon by confining himself to the categories of mysticism and magic must once again be totally led astray. For this community knows itself to be not only bound up with the saving history of the past, rooted in it and living in it, but also essentially looking forward to a salvation which is yet to come. The *Ecclesia* as the fellowship of the Messiah is itself Messianic: its existence can be properly described only by using the categories of eschatology, or expectation of a transcendent consummation. This consummation has dawned with Jesus; in His incarnate life it has already begun, for *ephthasen gar he basileia*—the Kingdom of God has come:[2] the rule of God for which all are looking is already among you, for He the transcendent eternal Messiah is already in their midst.[3] But as yet it was a concealed presence. Only with the

[1] Gal. 2:20. [2] Matt. 12:28; Luke 11:20. [3] Luke 17:21; Matt. 18:20.

Resurrection did the veil begin to be withdrawn. His presence among them as the Risen One is a transcendent happening, "realized eschatology" (4). The new age has now dawned. And yet, at the same time, it remains unfulfilled; in its plenitude it has still to be awaited. This expectation of the future consummation as distinguished from the salvation which has already been realized cannot be dismissed as a more or less ancillary element in the life of the Christian community; it is the very breath of its life (5). To live in this hope, in this tense expectation of the transcendent goal, and from that standpoint to view the here-and-now as a preliminary—that is precisely the fundamental character of the community's life. They "have, as though they had not".[1] And further: precisely this forward-looking attitude is identical with what they term the gift of the Holy Ghost. For He, the Holy Ghost, is the very life of the new age. *He* is the "realized eschatology". For they qualify the gift of the Holy Spirit as the first-fruits, the earnest, the pledge of the future. To be in the Spirit and to live in this expectation are one and the same thing. Therefore they know that their material life on earth, in this sinful body, subjected to the sinful ordinances of this world and chained to the body of this death, is a not-yet-having. They are therefore pilgrims on earth, they know that this earthly life is but a provisional dispensation which will not be transformed into the finality of eternal heavenly life until the Lord comes again in glory.

They walk as yet "by faith, not by sight".[2] As yet by faith—one must remember what faith means to these first Christians in order to measure the significance of the fact that precisely to this word, which sums up the whole gift of salvation, they add an "as yet". It is just life in the Spirit which is life on the threshold—one foot has already passed it, the other is still here. Of course, this paradoxical combination of the "not as yet" with the "but already" is expressed in various parts of the New Testament with very varying emphases: sometimes the accent falls on the "not yet", at other times on the "but already"; but the fact that every "not yet" is always also a

---

[1] 1 Cor. 7:29f.   [2] 2 Cor. 5:7.

"but already" and vice versa, is common to them all (6). Everywhere it is implied that the new life is a life on the threshold, and everywhere it is just the possession of the Holy Spirit which determines and characterizes that life on the threshold.

The spiritual is the eschatological and the eschatological is the spiritual. The fact of standing at a determinative point in the unfolding *historical* process of salvation is therefore the most essential characteristic of this "mysticism", just as the consciousness of the provisional is the decisive feature of this "magical" element (7).

We have already seen how, out of this mysticism and magic which are primarily and principally none other than faith and hope, there arose that unique life of fellowship which is characterized by the conscious paradox that it is essentially a fellowship of persons and not an institution. This is so in spite of the interior economy as a result of which each one is assigned his special function without there being any official recognition of distinctive rank.

Therefore this economy is something quite spontaneous, springing up of itself, something of which one is hardly aware. It is for this reason that we hear so little of it in the New Testament. When, however, it is spoken of, then the allusion occurs, not as describing a form of church administration, but as relating the parable of the body which has many members, and in connection with the teaching on the Holy Ghost. The description of this economy reaches its climax in the hymn of love,[1] which again culminates in the eschatological vision of faith becoming dissolved in sight. "Church order" as such has not the slightest importance in itself; it is as much a matter of course as is the functioning of his bodily organism for a healthy man.

Ministries have as yet acquired nothing of the character of offices. The command given by the Master Himself—"Whosoever would be great among you, let him be your servant"[2] —is lived out as the essential truth of things. Even the apostle who founded the community at Corinth and who received the

[1] 1 Cor. 12; 1 Cor. 13.   [2] Matt. 20:26f.

58

most explicit instruction on these matters, thinks it not beneath his dignity to strive to win the approval of his congregation and declined to exercise dominion over them.[1] He wishes to prove anew to them his apostleship, which in fact needed no further authentication, by the manifestation of the signs of an apostle.[2] And those in Corinth who are obviously marked out as leaders by their possession of the *charisma* and *diakonia* of *kybernein* (governing) are recalled to the community as persons who have proved themselves by faithful service, and who therefore have shown by their service that they are worthy to be obeyed when necessary.[3]

The tendency to exalt the office as such could not arise as long as men's hearts and hopes were set upon the future and in consequence the present dispensation regarded as provisional merely. The emergence of ecclesiastical rule and jurisdiction is coincident with the loss or weakening of the community's messianic consciousness. Both the pneumatic and the messianic factors work in the same direction. As long as they are sufficiently alive, they prevent and render superfluous all institutional consolidation. The community which waits in hope for the return of the Lord and which lives by faith and love in the possession of His Spirit, cannot be an institution, a church.

---

[1] 2 Cor. 1:24.   [2] 2 Cor. 12:12.   [3] 1 Cor. 16:15f.

Chapter Seven

DIVINE SERVICE, THE LIFE OF THE "ECCLESIA"

(a) *Cult and daily life*

Both in classical Greek and in the usage of the Greek Old Testament, *Ecclesia* means congregation, the assembled people. So then the New Testament *Ecclesia*, in its original form, is the fellowship of Christ or the people of God assembled for purposes of divine worship. Yet it would be incorrect to say of the *Ecclesia* that it becomes real only in the act of assembly (1); such a view would in fact fail to do justice to one of its most vital characteristics. For the first Christians were conscious of their membership of the *Ecclesia* even when the latter was not assembled for the cult. They understood their life to be a continuous act of worship apart from the cult altogether, when each individual in his particular walk in life, in the everyday world, in the family circle or in his daily avocation, offered his life to Christ his Master as a sacrifice, well-pleasing to God[1] (2). It is true nevertheless that their cultic assembly for the common hearing of the word, for the prayer of fellowship, and for the celebration of the sacrament served in a special way to make them increasingly aware of themselves as the *Ecclesia*, as the people of God made one with Christ and knit together through Him.

We may go further and say that these meetings of worship had precisely the dominating purpose of building up the Body of Christ (3). The assemblies were edifying, not in our colourless sense of the word, but in the strict and literal sense of building up. In this sense, of course, specific cultic acts of worship take precedence of the more general life of worship and witness in the world: for only here occurred the actual realization of the Body's communion in Christ which is the

[1] Rom. 12:1.

presupposition for the reality and witness of each individual's membership in the isolation of his worldly calling.

But it was not only the act of meeting in itself which was so significant for the realization of the individual's membership of the Body of Christ, it was rather the character of the meeting which served this very real purpose of incorporation. These meetings were not merely—as they came to be called later—a *coetus fidelium*, a coming together and a being with each other, but they aimed at making out of the mere assembly an act of vital co-operation.[1] They signified the performance of something in fellowship, a reciprocal giving and taking.[2] Only so can we appreciate the centrality of the so-called sacraments in such gatherings (4).

We may leave undecided the controversial issue of New Testament scholarship as to whether there were two types of service or only one; that is, one for preaching and prayer and another for sacramental worship, or whether every service as a matter of course included a celebration of the sacrament (5); for even if the latter should be found to be the case, the service must still have been divided into two parts in one of which unbelievers could share and in the other of which, of course, the faithful alone participated. Whether, therefore, this inevitable division implied a duality of service is in the last analysis of no consequence. It is, however, of some importance to note that even a meeting—or a part of one— devoted exclusively to the Word and prayer as opposed to a common meal (as for example Paul describes it in 1 Cor. 14) followed such a course and was of such a character that co-operative action in fellowship might be regarded as its decisive feature. It is especially emphasized that *all* were active in it. What we have already discovered concerning the intrinsic structure of the community, namely, that it knows no distinction between the active and the passive, between those who administer and those who are recipients—this is evinced anew in the character of divine worship. Each made his con-

---

[1] 1 Cor. 14.
[2] Luther's formula: *mutuum colloquium et consolatio fratrum* (Schmalk, Art. 111, IV).

tribution and for this very reason no one was allowed to monopolize the hearing of the assembly. Thus every one could have his turn.[1] This cult, therefore, knows nothing of the distinction between priests and laymen; its members are aware that they form a priesthood[2] and this holy priesthood is built up of each and all.[3] This does not first become true of the Pauline community, it is already true of the primitive Jerusalem church. Not only is the *koinonia* stressed here as an important aspect of the fellowship alongside of exhortation, prayer and the breaking of bread, it is also emphasized that prayer is uttered aloud with one accord.[4]

But this "religious" assembly contains from the very beginning a certain element of tension, about the nature and extent of which we must be clear. The climax of the meeting was reached in an act which, on the one hand, emphasized unmistakably the "cultic" in contradistinction to the profane; on the other hand, it took a feature of everyday life, the meal—and in fact a real eating in common[5]—as its special token of the holy. The pre-eminently cultic is therefore at the same time the pre-eminently everyday, non-cultic. The determination to do away with the opposition between sacred and profane, between the Sunday fellowship and the earthly realities of the workaday world, is revealed also in the fact that the whole life of each individual member revolves around the same centre as does this communal meal, namely, the connection with the sacrificial death of Christ; and from that centre it becomes consecrated as a living sacrifice and a service of God.[6]

It may therefore be affirmed that the *Ecclesia* refuses to admit the normative distinction, or rather opposition, prevalent in all other religions, between the sacred and profane, and instead abolishes it precisely in the central feature of its cultic worship. The whole life of the Christian is a worship of God and in the entire range of his existence he must therefore prove himself to be a member of the Body of Christ. The primitive Christian community of Jerusalem furnished a

---

[1] 1 Cor. 14:31. [2] 1 Pet. 2:9. [3] 1 Pet. 2:5.
[4] Acts 4:24. [5] 1 Cor. 11:20f. [6] Rom. 12:2.

specially striking demonstration of this desire to transcend the division between the sacred and the profane by its decision to have all things common; that is, by the abolition of the distinction between private and communal existence at the crucial point, where the right of private property is asserted. Of course, this does not mean that there was anything in the nature of a systematic communism; for it lay within the free choice of the individual as to how far he should surrender his property. But the mere fact of this experiment shows a resolute conviction about the inner necessity of overcoming the traditional opposition between the two zones, the sacred and profane, the religious day and the working day (6).

And yet, the tension was there. Before it had received the technical name of *Agape*, and before it had become the definitely profane or mundane act of feeding the poor and as such had freed itself from the Eucharist, the solemn meal was quite clearly a cultic act; it was in some sense from the very beginning what later was known specifically as a sacrament, and therefore had always about it the character of the esoteric, of something strictly confined to the initiated. On the other hand, the character of this rite was marked by such a natural matter-of-fact quality, was so closely bound up with the everyday, with the act of eating in common—as the disciples had been daily accustomed to do with their Master—that it might well be understood to suggest a desire to preclude anything in the nature of a cultic mystery. The solemn meal implies that the everyday world is wrought into the texture of saving history, and that saving history is implanted in the thick of everyday life.

The ritual meal was specially holy and solemn for the first Christians because it signified the presence of the Lord in the breaking of bread and the drinking of wine. It was edificatory in a special sense because just here, as nowhere else, the community became aware of itself as the Body of Christ.[1]

Whether or not there was from the beginning a conscious connection with the passion and death of the Lord, it is in-

---

[1] I Cor. 10:17.

conceivable that in such a cult the disciples should not have remembered the last meal which the Lord took with them on the eve of His crucifixion. But we ought to lay stress on that other thought which has become lost to our ecclesiastical tradition, namely, that for the early Christians—at any rate those of the apostolic community at Jerusalem—this mystery was penetrated with the recollection that on such an occasion the Risen Lord had appeared to them.[1] His eternal presence, much more than His death, the conquest of death through the resurrection much more than the atoning character of His passion, was the central feature of it. Therefore "they brake bread with gladness".[2] Thus arises the thought that in the ritual meal more than anywhere the community experienced the living presence of the Risen Lord in its midst (7).

Precisely when we see things from this point of view do we realize that the most holy is the most familiar. The solemn meal was of course merely the repetition of what the disciples, when they were with the Lord in the flesh, had daily experienced as a simple matter-of-fact reality; just as they had trod with Him the dusty roads of Galilee, and at times had washed with Him their soiled feet before eating[3] (8) so had they shared bread with Him, which He had broken, and drunk wine which He had blessed. What could be more straightforward, more usual, less mysterious than just this? And this was the very centre and climax of their divine worship, the form in which the highest and holiest was embodied: the self-manifestation of the Lord. One must see both aspects of this rite, its everyday quality and its solemnity, in order to become aware of the Church in its uniqueness and to understand how it might be that, just at this point, pre-eminently, the displacement of the *Ecclesia* by the Church could occur.

(b) *The Sacraments*

The sacramental meal—there can be no doubt about this—is that portion, or that form, of divine worship from which unbelievers were excluded. It is in a quite special way—what

---

[1] So especially Luke 24:13ff.; 36ff.   [2] Acts 2:46f.
[1] John 13:1ff.

is true of the cult as a whole—edification, the building up of the Body of Christ. It is therefore especially that which constitutes the Christian community as such: fellowship in and through Christ. It is, in fact, what is expressly said of it: *Koinonia somatos Christou*, a common sharing in the Body of Christ.[1] Not there exclusively, but there intensively, the *Ecclesia* is constituted as the fellowship of Christ, becomes in a deeply significant way *Ecclesia Christou* (9). At this point divine materialism and divine socialism unite: for in the eating of the bread and in the drinking of the wine it happens that Christ is in their midst and in consequence they become one body. Here therefore we see in operation the mystical— the unification of all in the One—and the magical—the communication of spiritual power through a material instrument. Is that a sacrament and if so, in what sense? Before we answer this question, let us turn to the other sacred rite which from the beginning was practised in the Church and which likewise belonged to the very essence of the Christian community, namely, baptism.

We are not chiefly concerned with its historical origin; we take as our point of departure the fact that we hear of the Church only as a community which was accustomed to practise this rite as a rite of initiation. Paul gives us the classical theological interpretation of baptism, but it would surely be wrong to imagine that this theology existed from the beginning and was universally accepted as the presupposition for baptism or for the reception of the gift believed to be imparted in baptism. Baptism is not in the first instance a cognitive but a causative act; in baptism one received the gift of the Holy Ghost (10). The rite of baptism belongs entirely to that sphere of pneumatic, dynamic happenings, which has been discussed above (in Ch. 5). Something *happened* to the newly baptized person, in that para-logical, hence para-theological sense, to wit, in the sense that this event was not necessarily dependent upon the acceptance of a specific theological interpretation such as Paul expounds. Through the

[1] 1 Cor. 10:16.

ceremony of baptism as such, something of the power of the Holy Ghost entered into the baptized person. One may term this conception magical—but what more is suggested than that God used this external human action in order to give man a share in the gift which constituted the very life of the *Ecclesia*? Whether adults only were baptized or children and even babies too is quite a subordinate issue. In any case there could easily arise from the Old Testament rite of initiation—circumcision—which baptism superseded, and from the idea of the covenant, which was always thought of in connection with whole families rather than isolated individuals, such an interpretation of baptism as would make possible the baptism of children (11). The New Testament leaves us in complete uncertainty on this matter. On the other hand, it is clear that for the understanding of baptism as interpreted by Paul, intellectual activities are required of which not only no baby but also no small child would be capable. But Paul nowhere says that this interpretation, this deeper understanding of baptism, is the *conditio sine qua non* of its performance or even of its efficacy for the imparting of the Spirit; the Pauline teaching does, however, suggest that the full sense of Baptism can only be realized where it is understood as a dying with Christ and therefore where Christ's death as having taken place for our salvation is believed in (12).

In the New Testament these two rites, which the later Church called sacraments, have nothing to do with Church order. No word is said as to who may or may not baptize or about the administration of bread and wine in the meal. And yet here, in these so-called sacraments, lies the starting point for the later institutional development, for the movement by which the early Christian community becomes a Church. Why so? Baptism and the Lord's Supper are, so it seems at least, institutions. The question which, in face of these two rites, forces itself upon our attention, is this: Why is it necessary to be baptized in order to attain membership of the community and therewith a share in the saving gift which has been granted it? Why is it necessary that the society should perform the rite of the meal in order to realize the full presence of its Lord and so to become in the fullest sense the Body of Christ?

Of course, we cannot help seeing in the light of Pauline theology the deeper meaning of these rites, their intimate connection with the centre of the faith, with the vicarious passion and death of the Lord. Baptism means that, and so does the supper; but why should there be any need for this special form of a ritual action? Does not the Christian possess in the Word, without the aid of these special rites, that which they convey? And if so—why then this duplication and why the special distinction of these particular rites? Here we seem to reach a point where a certain limit is set to the spiritual freedom of the community. Here we are confronted by a surd, which, like the mystery of the *Ecclesia* itself, cannot be simply deduced from the fact of Christ as announced in the Word and apprehended by faith—something downright positive, laid down, something the justification of which can only be expressed by saying: it is so ruled, so ordained, so given—in other words an institution, whose givenness in the last resort is its sole authorization. These rites must so be—thus, broadly speaking, it seems to be the case—because they go back to the institution of Jesus Himself.

Augustine and, in his succession, the Reformers tried to complete this merely positivistic answer by a naturalistic explanation, in that they termed the sacraments the *verbum visibile* and argued that this special mode of communication was conditioned by the necessities of our sensuous nature. The mere word does not suffice, we need such concrete representation, the visible language of signs. While there is a certain measure of truth in this argument, however, it is not absolutely satisfying in itself, the less so as there is not the slightest trace of any grounds for it to be found in the New Testament itself. It is obviously an afterthought, a theological-psychological rationalization of something simply given, and to that extent irrational.

Another line of thought should bring us nearer to New Testament realities.

Through these two rites the individual is joined to the real and concrete congregation of the faithful in such a way as could not happen—at least not so unmistakably—through the mere word of preaching. One can listen to the announcement of the divine Word without belonging to the community, without identifying oneself with it, abiding in it, and taking part in its life. The so-called sacraments are the *verbum communale*, the form of the Word through which the individual is really incorporated and made one with the community. The complementary aspect as it were of the same matter is that through these rites there finds expression the truth that the fellowship of Jesus is grounded in an *action* of God, which takes place in the real historical world, and for the completion of which God uses the Christian community. The sacrament is the *verbum activum*. The communion of Christ is realized through a common action of the congregation, and is realized in the congregation. To this corresponds the historical fact that it was the so-called sacraments which gradually, more than anything else, erected a breakwater against the tide of individualistic enthusiasm and so held the community together as a community.

There is still another and final consideration, through which alone the appearance of a merely positive order—that it is so and must be so because it has been so ordained—is first fully eliminated. The Last Supper, as celebrated by the community, is not merely a symbol, a symbolic representation of the atoning passion and death of Christ; it is an integral part of this saving act itself. The Last Supper, as Jesus celebrated it with His disciples, is a part of the events of the Passion and indeed that part in which Jesus constituted the body of His disciples as the nucleus of the New Covenant.[1] In sight of His imminent death upon the Cross, Jesus brake bread with His disciples and handed them the cup, as a token of the New Covenant founded in His death. The Saviour's act of self-oblation and the founding of the Christian community are not symbolically, but really, connected with this rite. Of course, the bread and wine are only signs of what was meant, since Jesus Himself is still amongst them in the flesh (13)[2] but

---

[1] See above, p. 23.   [2] Mark 14:22f.

in and through these signs the Lord had pledged Himself to the community and in the reception of these signs the believing and understanding disciples have been re-born to live in communion with Him and with each other.[1] This Last Supper means the birth-pangs of the community springing from the Crucified. Therefore it is not an "as if", but the very substance of saving history.

When now, after the death of the Lord, the community celebrates this meal, it does so not simply in order to recollect something which once happened, but also in the certainty that what happened once is now being repeated; for it knows that He Himself is present in its midst in the eating of the bread and drinking of the wine and that thereby it is fashioned anew as a communion—both a communion with Christ and of one member with another. It is precisely in this act of communion that there really takes place, ever afresh, the creation of the Christian community. In this happening, the Lord Himself is the real initiator. His action consists in His self-disclosure, and in thus manifesting Himself He reunites His own to Himself and to each other, mediating His action through their common rite. That which happens to the *Ecclesia* through the whole range of its cultic worship, namely, the upbuilding of the community, happens here in an intensive form, in that act which is only possible as a communal act and in which the individual, ever anew, is incorporated into the body, appropriating the saving benefits of the death of Jesus (14). Only it is no longer now as formerly a farewell meal, laden with all the pain and sadness of the hour of separation; it is above all a meal of festive joy celebrated by those who are united with the Conqueror of sin and death. While the celebrants from one point of view look back to the past, still more do they look forward to the future, to that meal to which the Lord had already alluded— the festal meal of the Kingdom consummated beyond the horizon of death.[2] Therefore the Last Supper is something very different from an institution: it is the performance of an act of fellowship—of the fellowship centred in Christ and

---

[1] I Cor. 10:16.   [2] Mark 14:25 and parallels.

grounded in the saving history of the past, present and future. It is the characteristic form of Christian communion and worship, taking its special impress from the passion of the Christ, therefore the proper, specifically Christian form of worship, a ritual edification of the Christian community implying the background of saving history (15).

What now is the position with regard to baptism? That it too is intended as an act of real as opposed to merely symbolical incorporation—*incorporatio*—was a conclusion reached in our previous discussion. Its characteristic distinction from the Last Supper lies in the fact that it can happen only once. Whereas in the Last Supper it is emphasized that the individual must be united to the Body ever anew, baptism emphasizes that this incorporation takes place as an initial act and once for all. Through it the individual decisively separates himself from the surrounding heathen world, confesses his allegiance to the community which admits him, becomes a member of the Body of Christ. But the question remains: why must this event assume just this form of baptism, of being baptized? Why should the gift of the Holy Spirit be conveyed through just this external medium? Precisely the same considerations apply here as in the case of the Last Supper, except that here the relation to the saving history itself is not so obvious. And yet we may affirm: baptism too belongs to the story of the Christ in that Jesus allowed Himself to be baptized by John the Baptist. For from the standpoint of the Cross the early Church must have realized that baptism was an act whereby Jesus vicariously assumed the sins of the world.[1] Jesus took upon Himself the sins of His people and allowed Himself to be cleansed as though He needed such cleansing. He identified Himself with the sins of others (16).

Thus understood, the baptism of Jesus is in point of fact the basis for the soteriological significance of His death: for only in virtue of that act of identification has His death saving power for us. Thus baptism, too, as the rite of initiation into the community is inextricably associated with the facts of saving history, as Paul teaches. Whether or not the individual

[1] Matt. 3:15; John 1:31ff.

70

to be baptized realizes this is not of decisive importance: what is important is that baptism was understood in this sense by the early Church—a sense imprinted upon it by Christ Himself—and that the community can receive the individual only on the basis of such an interpretation. One can share in the life of the *Ecclesia* only in virtue of what took place in the vicarious baptism of Jesus, and one can be united with Jesus only through union with the *Ecclesia* and membership of its body. In baptism the individual becomes identified with the Christ who vicariously assumes the sins of His people, and, through this sharing in His death, becomes a member of His mystical body. Therefore baptism likewise is not an institution, not something which has been simply ordained thus. It is, in a different way from the Last Supper, but yet in the same sense and for the same reason a real act of assimilation to the community; it is not a passive sign, but a real event mediated through an efficacious symbolic act.

Just as we cannot conceive of any act of worship in which all the necessary elements—the common act in fellowship, the foundation in saving history and the real union with Him and with each other—are so perfectly combined as in the Last Supper, so no form of initiation into the community is conceivable where the various moments—of confession, penance, and communion rooted in saving history—are so harmoniously expressed as in baptism. Every suggestion of the merely contingent, the inexplicable command, has disappeared. In baptism and the Lord's Supper, the community completes the process by which it realizes itself as a community.

In conclusion, however, we must add a word, in the opposite sense, as it were. Intimately as these two so-called sacraments are associated with the saving events in Christ, yet they are not identical with them—they are not therefore unconditionally necessary to salvation. In asserting their unconditional necessity to salvation, we should be contradicting the witness of the New Testament. One can speak of salvation in Christ apart from these two rites. One can believe in Christ and in salvation through Him without sharing in these rites. The community of Jesus does not first become a reality through them; it is already a reality. These symbolic rites are given to it that it mey preserve the life which it has independently of them. The "where two or three are gathered together in my Name there am I in the midst of them"[1] is still valid and real where there is no celebration of the Lord's Supper. The Reformers have therefore correctly understood the meaning of Scripture, in allowing to these sacraments only a *necessitas relativa*, not a *necessitas absoluta*, while at the same time earnestly emphasizing their high significance. The decisive test of one's belonging to Christ is not reception of baptism, nor partaking in the Lord's Supper, but solely and exclusively a union with Christ through faith which shows itself active in love.

It is doubtless correct to say that the "sacraments" belong to the inner life and essential nature of the Christian fellowship —so much so in fact that we may assert that it gains strength and solidarity through them. But they do not produce it. They are given to it, but it does not spring into existence through them. The community comes to be through the Word and Spirit of Jesus Christ, which we receive in faith. Therefore "sacraments" are not the centre of the New Testament message, even though they are not far from that centre (17). The category under which they may be classified is lacking in the New Testament. It has not yet occurred to the community that these two rites, later called sacraments, belong together and constitute a special feature. A peculiar distinction, such as is implied in the concept "sacrament", is not given to them in the New Testament. In confirmation of this we may point to the straightforward juxtaposition of the four cultic elements which are to be found in the primitive Jerusalem community:[2] the teaching of the apostles, the *Koinonia*, the breaking of bread, and prayer. Again, the same thing is attested by the fact that no words are lost in discussing who shall be authorized to perform the rites. Properly speaking, New Testament Christianity knows nothing of the word "sacrament", which belongs essentially to the heathen world of the Graeco-Roman empire and which unfortunately some

[1] Matt. 18:20.   [2] Acts 2:42.

of the Reformers unthinkingly took over from ecclesiastical tradition. For this word, and still more the overtones which it conveys, is the starting point for those disastrous developments which began soon to transform the community of Jesus into the Church which is first and foremost a sacramental Church.

Chapter Eight

So far our thesis has proved sound: the *Ecclesia* of the New Testament is a communion of persons and nothing else. It is the Body of Christ, but not an institution. Therefore it is not yet what it later became as the result of a slow, steady, hence unnoticed process of transformation: it is not yet a Church. The Church—firstly the early catholic, then the neo-catholic Roman church—is distinguished from the *Ecclesia* above all in this—that it is no longer primarily a communion of persons, but rather an institution, and—particularly in its Roman Catholic form—understands itself as such. How did this transformation come about? It must first of all be pointed out that we should not expect to find a single event with which the spirit of primitive Christianity suddenly ceases to exist and the new phenomenon of the Church begins. The ecclesiastical development of the community of Jesus Christ is so difficult a conundrum precisely because the change takes place in tiny but continuous stages, and indeed at first in such a way that even the new institutional elements are not simply innovations but in actual fact —as Catholic theories assert—"develop" from obscure origins which are already partly latent in the New Testament *Ecclesia*. (1) If our thesis is to be substantiated it must be possible to show that these elements already existing in the New Testament do not belong to the essential character of the *Ecclesia* but rather stand in opposition to it. We shall see that in point of fact it is a question of a number of such elements, not of any single one, and that these are simultaneously developed and commingled in such a way that the net result represents the new phenomenon: the Church. Nevertheless it is possible to locate a point which might be regarded as the real point of departure for the emergence and crystallization

74

of the new tendencies. That point—and this is what makes it so truly sinister—lies very near to the centre of the New Testament *Ecclesia*, and the change which takes place here consists in a very slight shift of emphasis which can be characterized by saying that what was very near to the centre becomes itself the centre: namely, the sacred meal, the Eucharist. From being an act, perpetually repeated according to the Word of the Lord, by which the community seeks to realize itself as a fellowship with and in Christ, the festal meal becomes the essence of salvation itself and the thing which constitutes the community's life. While the Lord had given it in order to emphasize the Word and Spirit through which He Himself is present, it now became the real decisive self-disclosure of the divine, depriving the Word of its centrality and therefore to an ever-increasing extent imparting to the meal itself the character of a holy thing; a process in the course of which the substantial physical elements, which originally had no independent significance and were only signs having meaning merely as the material basis of the rite, became the real media of God's self-communication. (2) In such a way the holy meal first became the "sacrament" and so the focal point of faith.

In this were implied a series of further changes fraught with momentous consequences. In the earliest period no importance was attached to the unity of the local Christian community, since the *Ecclesia* exists wherever two or three are gathered together in His name, and the idea of a local community as such had simply not yet arisen; (3) but now that the sacramental meal is of the essence of the Christian society, the unity of the local community becomes immediately the indispensable condition of correct celebration. (4) The plurality of house-churches must of necessity disappear, the principle "in one place only one congregation" is formulated, the local community springs up as a stone in the fabric of the greater whole, the collective Church. Therefore since the meal is now regarded as that which constitutes the life of the Christian community, the concrete congregation which celebrates this meal must be the real Church of Christ. Secondly, this necessary unit and uniqueness of the local community could only be realized or assured, if someone established and embodied it in his own person. From the circle of overseers (*episcopoi*) or presbyters to whom had ever been entrusted the duty of ordering and guiding the life of the community, one must now emerge as the authoritative leader, in whose person the unity of the Christian communion was visibly represented, and who was responsible for securing it: "the" bishop. Thirdly, once the Eucharist had become the food of salvation, it was inevitable that the distinction between those who give and those who receive should henceforth receive an important religious emphasis, whereas previously it had been a merely technical arrangement without any religious significance. A distinction between the priesthood and the laity began to become marked. Fourthly, with the death of the first, the apostolic, generation, the need made itself felt to obtain a substitute for apostolic authority. What could be more natural than the transference of this authority to the priest-bishops, who in any case were exalted as authorities by their priestly pre-eminence over the mass of the laity and their significance for the unity of the local church?

These various developments, however, acquired their supreme importance only because in the *Ecclesia* itself a fundamental though as yet hardly perceptible change had taken place through the over-valuation of the sacred meal. Previously it had been the work of the Holy Spirit which had imparted to the congregation its organic life: it was a *spiritual* unity and precisely as such the Body of Christ. But now it had become a *sacramental* unity. That personal fellowship which had characterized the earlier period was no longer necessary in order to receive and enjoy in common the benefits of the sacramental food of salvation. Salvation has beome a sacred thing and this sacred thing is bestowed by those who administer, the priests, and is received by the others—the laymen. The Body of Christ is now no longer the communion itself but is becoming increasingly identified with the elements of the holy meal. Now Christians belong to each other no longer through the creative Word springing from the revela-

76

tion in Christ and through the action of the Holy Spirit stirring the depths of the heart and dissolving the selfish isolation of the individual. Since the sacramental food becomes the essential thing, the *Ecclesia* is transformed from a spiritual *koinonia*, a unity of persons, into a unity flowing from common relationship to a thing, that is, into a collective. It is no longer the fruit of the *Agape*, the self-imparting love of God, which binds individuals to each other through a real gift of the Holy Ghost, but it has become that miraculous thing, the sacrament, which the members share with each other; they now *receive* the Body of Christ, instead of *being* the Body of Christ. Now they receive the divine salvation as a heavenly medicine, a *pharmakon athanasias*, a means of spiritual healing which conveys the gift of eternal life.

One cannot over-estimate the importance of this change from a spiritual communion with its utterly personal character into a sacramental collective with its essentially impersonal centre and therefore impersonal structure, even though the change may have come about not at once, but on the contrary very slowly, in small imperceptible stages. Only when taken in conjunction with this change do the above-mentioned four points acquire their decisive significance. We must see the two movements—sacramentalism and institutionalism—as interlocked and developing concomitantly in order to be able to understand each of them separately. Institutionalism is produced by sacramentalism. Episcopacy is exalted through the emphasis laid on sacraments, and only from the sacramental point of view can we understand why precisely the office of bishop was valued and why it was valued to such an extent (5).

To be fair it must be said that the office did not attain this degree of importance through sacramental development only; rather there exists also a root of institutionalism which is— probably—independent of the latter, and which on the contrary favoured the growth of sacramentalism by its glorification of the office. It has been pointed out above how already in the primitive community of Jerusalem there existed tendencies towards an authoritative church government which

77

rested upon a very natural and almost inevitable misconception of the nature of apostolic authority. They were still nothing more than tendencies which, in a decisive hour, through the might of the Word and Spirit of Jesus Christ active in the apostle Paul, it had been possible to render innocuous. Faced by the power of the truth as it is in Christ, the false, formalistic authority of the pillars—springing from a radical misunderstanding—could not assert itself, and collapsed. But the tendency remained; it had not been erased by that event. It was therefore only to be expected that it would reappear, and in short, in proportion as the spirit of Christ lost its overwhelming power in the community, would more and more come into its own.

Such a development can be plainly observed at the very close of the apostolic period. The first epistle of Clement, written at the turn of the first century, shows us how, with the backing of Rome, the principle of the formal quasi-legal authority of the episcopal office was successfully maintained at Corinth. (6) This writing formulates the rule that persons who have once been elected to such an office possess in perpetuity the right to exercise it and that this right must be recognized by the Christian community. The way in which Clement calls the Corinthian church to order can hardly be distinguished from the way in which Paul exhorted the Corinthians to respect the tried and tested overseer[1]—and yet a world of difference lies between the two; Paul refers to the self-authentication of those leading men through their service and urges the community not to deny recognition to those who have proved themselves. Clement on the other hand refers to the legal right which has been secured through installation in the office. What here becomes visible at a certain point in the development of the *Ecclesia* was not an isolated case, but rather was symptomatic of a movement which was everywhere beginning in the Church. The spiritual structure of the community begins to give place to a legal one. What happens from the sacramental angle in regard to the structure of the community, happens at the same time

[1] I Cor. 16:16.

and in the same sense from the point of view of the office: from the personal fellowship there develops an institution, from the *koinonia*, a collective; from the organism—the Body of Christ—there develops the apparatus of ecclesiastical authority.

The two movements—the institutional and the sacramental—stimulate each other and unite to produce their final effect. The priest-bishop becomes an apostolic authority. The presbyters and overseers, from being proved servants, become simply personages occupying the place of honour, but from among them there emerges the bishop as "the" leader and embodiment of the unity of the Church. Already on the edge of the New Testament itself—in the pastoral epistles—there is faintly outlined this movement which culminates in the monarchical episcopate and its authoritarianism. It is this development—and not the one which the Johannine writings show to have existed simultaneously, and to have been of the reverse order, anti-official, anti-authoritarian—which was predestined to prevail in the course of the struggle with the gnostic heresies. At this stage the imperative need is for what is firm, of a juridical character, authoritative: the *Ecclesia* must become the Church if it is to win in this struggle. But the fact that it was just with the figure of the bishop that this tendency to legalistic hardening was connected, may be explained simply and solely by the shift in the focal point of the Christian community itself, which happened quite independently of the militant attitude required of the Church in the world; by the misunderstanding of the meal as a sacrament, as the real medium of salvation. So it is the priest-bishop to whom the growing Church in its need of authority clings, and to whom is imputed the authority that seems so necessary. But this authority could be no other than that of the early apostolate. The bishop now becomes the successor of the apostles; the theory of the apostolic succession of the bishops takes shape.

This theory which doubtless was not a pure fiction but possessed at least a good *fundamentum in re* (7) involved a further modification: the bishop becomes the guarantor of apostolic doctrine. In the New Testament *Ecclesia* there was no special connection between the overseers or presbyters and the function of teaching, of preaching the Word. The persons appointed to have control of the churches were marked out by the *charisma* of *kybernesis*, not by that of preaching or teaching. Persons of quite another order had the chief responsibility for the service of the Word: the apostles in the first instance, then the prophets, the teachers and the evangelists. Not until the end of the apostolic period, in the pastoral epistles, do we find the bishop appearing as especially responsible for the preaching of the Word—at a time when already he is named in the singular, in other words, when the monarchical episcopate is already beginning to be constituted. With this change of function there may well have been connected a development of the greatest significance, about the history of which we know almost nothing: namely, ordination, the transmission of a special grace by the laying on of hands.

The laying on of hands plays a part of great importance in the New Testament, especially in the Acts of the Apostles. Yet nowhere do we see it in connection with the transference of a special function or office. When at a later date we find the Greek word *cheirotonein* or *cheirotonia* employed in this sense, we are faced by a linguistic usage which is completely unknown in the New Testament itself. There *cheirotonein* has nothing whatever to do with the laying on of hands; it is the *terminus technicus* for "to choose", "appoint to an office", and the underlying idea is not the laying on of hands but the raising of the hand—the customary manner of denoting assent to the election of some particular candidate. Any sort of charismatic or sacramental conception is—within the New Testament period—in no sense associated therewith. But on the contrary the laying on of hands is an action by the performance of which it was believed that the transmission of a special spiritual grace was effected. Through the laying on of hands the gift of the Holy Ghost is mediated to such as were already baptized;[1] through the laying on of hands

[1] Acts 8:17.

the pious Ananias restores sight to Paul.[1] With the laying on of hands Paul and Barnabas are sent out on their first missionary journey.[2] By the laying on of hands Paul imparts the Holy Ghost to twelve men at Ephesus.[3] Nowhere in connection with such incidents is there any thought of anything in the nature of an ordination. Only in the sub-apostolic pastoral epistles does the pseudonymous Paul remind his pupil Timothy[4] that through the laying on of hands—which according to 1 Tim. 4:14 had been performed not by the apostle himself but by the presbytery—he had received a special grace; what grace is not specified, but probably the allusion is to the gift which was to qualify him for his office.

If this be so, an enormously significant change of emphasis has taken place. In the earlier Pauline period, the theory was that a special type of ministry is assigned to any one who has received a gift of grace, a *charisma* of the Holy Ghost, which the Holy Ghost apportions to whomsoever He will.[5] Now the theory is that the gift of the Holy Spirit which qualifies for a specific office is dependent upon the laying on of hands, whether it be by an apostle or by the presbytery, and is assured by the performance of this rite. Only a small step is needed before we reach the formula of Cyprian: whoever has the office receives the spiritual grace requisite for its fulfilment. But the office is obtained through ordination by the laying on of hands. By the latter means, which from now on is named *cheirotonein*, it is possible to exercise control over the operations of the Spirit. Of course, in the act of ordination, the Holy Ghost is invoked (8), but one is already certain that, provided things are done correctly, the laying on of hands will infallibly secure the endowment of the Holy Ghost necessary for the performance of the office. This theory, which does not emerge until the close of the apostolic period, together with the practice of ordination, constitutes a further stage in the evolution from the rule of the Spirit characteristic of primitive Christianity to the fully developed hierocracy of the Church. At least in practice if not in theory one now

[1] Acts 9:17.   [2] Acts 13:3.   [3] Acts 19:6.
[4] 1 Tim. 4:14; 2 Tim. 1:6.   [5] 1 Cor. 12:11.

exercises a control over the Holy Spirit: by the rite of ordination the person appointed to the office is equipped with spiritual grace. One link only is missing in the chain: the transmission of the apostolic *charisma* to the bishop.

This last link is furnished by the idea, which later becomes a doctrine, that the bishops were installed in their office by the apostles. Now, of course, the New Testament several times records that the apostles themselves appointed presbyters—and we may even calmly add the Pauline term of overseer or "episcopos"[1]—to govern the Christian communities which they founded. But that is not true of all the churches—of which many indeed sprang into being without apostolic foundation—nor is it true in any special way of those among these presbyters or "episcopoi" who later emerged as monarchical bishops out of the mass of their brethren, and were now first regarded as true bishops in the sense which was subsequently attached to this term. To the office of bishop *in this sense* no apostle ever instituted any man. The lists of bishops published by Hegesippus, even supposing they reached back to apostolic times, do not therefore prove what they are intended to prove.

But that was not the point; the essential thing was that the bishop was believed to be the bearer of apostolic authority, and that his qualification for the office was made to depend upon his ordination by another bishop. The fictitious nature of this interpretation of apostolic succession occurred to no one, and the fact that the transmission of apostolic authority and apostolic *charisma* through ordination and the laying on of hands was an innovation (of which no traces are to be found in the New Testament)[2] was obviously concealed by the misunderstanding which in the meantime had arisen, namely, that *cheirotonein* means "to lay hands upon". It was sufficient that a means now existed of imparting apostolic authority and that by this means it became possible to increase the authority of the priest-bishop to the highest degree.

The transformation of the *Ecclesia* into the Church has

[1] Phil. 1:1.
[2] With the single exception of 2 Tim. 1:6, where, however, it is not a question of Timothy as a bishop.

therefore several roots, some of which lie in the soil of the New Testament itself. But it is certain that we are confronted by a transformation rather than a development, because the essential being of the *Ecclesia* as a spiritual unity, a communion of persons, has in the process been wrought into something else—an institution. The transformation of ministries into offices, of the meal into the sacrament which constitutes the life of the Church, that is, the institutional and sacramental motives, share equally in this development and react upon each other. The sacrament required priests, the need of order and unity required legal, canonical, authority. Both streams flowed together to produce the figure of the priest-bishop who possesses apostolic authority to teach and administrative authority for the regulation of church life. Episcopal rule and the administration of the sacraments as channels of saving grace condition each other mutually. The union of sacrament and office gives rise to the new sacrament of the office—ordination, which, when traced back to apostolic foundations, reveals a mingling of the old and new. Now it is the person of the priest-bishop, who, as authoritative vicar of Jesus Christ Himself, can distribute the salvation of Christ and claim for himself the obedience which believers owe to their Lord. The episcopal administration of a sacramental grace places the Christian community in the position of a receiving laity; episcopal apostolic authority makes of them subjects who owe obedience. Only through this two-fold dependence upon the Church ruled by bishops and priests can the individual attain salvation. Out of the "mystical" brotherhood rooted in the Word and the Spirit, out of the Body of Christ whose head is Christ Himself alone, and whose members therefore are of equal status, out of the royal priesthood and holy nation has grown the Church—a totality composed of individual communities, each of which comes under the ecclesiastical jurisdiction of a bishop, who as adminstering priest stands opposed to the receiving laity because he controls the sacrament, the food of salvation, the sacral thing which holds together the individual components and makes them into a solidary collective.

Chapter Nine

THE CHRISTIAN FELLOWSHIP AND THE RISE OF THE CHURCH

W e have learnt something of the *Ecclesia* of the New Testament in all its paradoxical and unique characteristics. The question arises whether this *Ecclesia* is a living actual reality or an idea. It is both. For the *Ecclesia* of which the apostles write is certainly the governing reality in which they live and move and to which they bear witness. But at the same time it is something they describe as the *true* Church, something that can only be imperfectly represented in the empirical world, something to which the actual realities of church life as manifested in Corinth, Colossae or Jerusalem stood again and again in a certain degree of tension, just as the new life of Christ which Paul characterizes in the 6th or the 8th chapter of the Epistle to the Romans stands in a relation of tension to the actual existence of this man who is a new creature endowed with supernatural grace and yet is imperfectly released from sin. The great word of Luther is true of the New Testament *Ecclesia* also. The countenance of the Church is the countenance of a sinner.[1]

And yet that which the apostles call *Ecclesia* is not a mere ideal but the reality in which as apostles of Jesus Christ they live, the reality apart from which their apostolic office and their whole Christian witness would cease to be effective; it is the objective reality corresponding to their subjective faith in Jesus Christ. The *Ecclesia* is the sphere of actual and realized fellowship with the Christ—a fellowship which is as real as their faith and love and hope are real. It is constituted by the fellowship in Christ of those who are united with each other through Christ and it is as real as is their zealous and brotherly love of each other, as are the sacrifices which they make to each other in money and property, time and strength, security and life.

[1] W.A., XL, 11, p. 560.

84

It is as real as are the prayers which they voice with one accord, as the songs with which they unite to praise God, as the meal of which they joyfully partake in communion with each other and in which they experience the presence of their Lord, as the Holy Ghost who for them is not a lofty ethereal idea, but a living energy producing miracles, the experienced power of God upon which their entire hopes for the future are based. The *Ecclesia* in the sense of the *koinonia Christou* and *koinonia pneumatos*—therefore also the Body of Christ—wherein the one Spirit bestows upon each his peculiar gift and therefore assigns to each his characteristic ministry; the *Ecclesia*, belief in which they profess, is reality, heavenly divine reality —and yet it is a treasure in earthen vessels, something which not only by those without, but by the faithful themselves was being perpetually misunderstood and effectually distorted. The wonder of divine grace was manifested, however, in the fact that these misunderstandings and distortions could again and again be overcome, and in the fact that ever afresh not merely the ideal but also the empirical Church triumphed over all too human misconceptions.

The *Ecclesia* of which the apostles speak was thus not simply a theory or ideal springing from the vision of Christ; it was also the sphere of the new life grounded in the historical fact of redemption through Jesus Christ, and in His effective presence and power as living Head of the body. When this is recognized it can be clearly seen how baseless is the reproach so often levelled against the view here put forward, that it does not take seriously the Incarnation of Jesus Christ in His Church. The opinion that the institutional Church is the Incarnation, that is, the concretely historical form, the form of a servant in which Jesus Christ is historically manifest, amounts to nothing less than a denial that the apostolic *Ecclesia* is a real fact of history. The New Testament writings with their picture of the *Ecclesia* show that the Lord created for himself a body which was certainly not a Church, but a spiritual communion of Persons. The opinion that to take seriously the Incarnation requires that one should vindicate ecclesiasticism and allow the historical Church to be the necessary embodiment of the exalted Lord overlooks the fact that He was truly embodied in the *Ecclesia*, but that this embodiment, the *Ecclesia*, had not the character which it later assumed: the character of an institution. It is to make a considerable *petitio principii* to postulate that the continued incarnation of the exalted Lord could only happen in the form of ecclesiastical institutional development, and it would be an assertion to which the New Testament itself gives the lie, and which can only be made by those who regard Church history as of greater importance than the New Testament witness.

We have seen in one of its critical stages the struggle which the true *Ecclesia* waged against human misconceptions during the period of primitive Christianity, and have noted the reflection of that struggle in the New Testament. We have seen also how in point of fact within the sphere of early New Testament Christianity there were current divergent interpretations of what constitutes the unity of the *Ecclesia*, interpretations as widely disparate as are for example the quasi-gnostic anti-authoritarian spirit of the Johannine writings on the one hand, and the quasi-Judaic, authoritarian theocratic attitude of the Jerusalem pillars on the other. But we realized too how these cleavages were again and again transcended by the triumphant unity of the Spirit and by the sincere Christian and brotherly love which in spite of all discords never allowed any disruption to materialize.

In this *Ecclesia* there were many varied streams. From the primitive Christian witness of the Jerusalem community, the Pauline and Johannine theologies had developed. From the primitive Christian, hardly recoverable, witness to the Resurrection which marked the genesis of Christianity in Jerusalem, there had grown both the Pauline affirmations and the very different kind of testimony which lies before us in the late reports of the synoptics. From the Jerusalem conception of the Christian community, still tied up with Judaism, there had sprung the Pauline thesis of freedom from the law, and also the Epistle to the Hebrews fashioned by such a contrasted outlook. But the remarkable thing is just this, that none of these tendencies prevailed to the exclusion of the others, so that at the end of the apostolic age we see on the one side, in the pastoral epistles, a conception of the *Ecclesia* approximating to Paul though at many points conflicting with his spirit and which, in spite of its superficial Paulinism, stands much nearer to the Judaistic spirit of the early Jerusalem community. Then again, on the other side, we see in the Johannine writings a point of view which refuses to allow any sort of authoritarian office, but takes as its norm for church life the spirit of mutual service in the sense of the footwashing scene.

There was just not *one* line of development—in the direction of later catholicism; any one who was acquainted with the New Testament only would never arrive at the supposition that from its matrix the later episcopal church would spring. Just as real was the other and opposite possibility that development would proceed in the direction indicated by the Johannine writings. This question therefore imperatively demands an answer: How was it then that in the event one tendency only—the tendency to develop a hierarchical church—prevailed? How came it about that just this conception of the *Ecclesia*, which in the New Testament existed only amongst other conceptions and at an embryonic stage, should in effect supplant all others and should lead finally to the complete structure of the Catholic Church, though at first of course, and for a long time, only to the structure of the early Catholic Church?

Three arguments are adduced in order to show, supposedly, that this particular line of development was inevitable.

(i) There came the period of the gnostic heresies with their unbridled individualism and enthusiasm, under the impact of which the *Ecclesia* was threatened at first with disruption, then with annihilation. It was essential for the *Ecclesia* to erect barriers against this torrent in the interests of its own security and self-preservation. It did so (a) by the establishment of a canon of apostolic writings as a counterblast to the canon of Marcion, who was half a gnostic; (b) by the drawing up of a firm rule of faith, the definition of dogma which

87

should be the official norm of all church teachers; (c) both these things could only be accomplished by the creation of a third—though essentially a primary—guarantee of unity and coherence, namely, the impregnable authoritative office, the apostolic-priestly office of bishop.

(a) We have already spoken about the necessity of constituting the apostolic testimony to Jesus Christ as the criterion of all further testimony.[1] If the Church wished to take seriously the idea of "tradition" and to preserve the original foundations, it could do no other than hold fast to the apostolic witness, in so far as this had been crystalized in written documents (1), and to establish it as a canon. We cannot be grateful enough to the developing church for securing this foundation.

(b) Even the definition of a rule of faith was not without real justification. Of course to call attention in this way to a minimal *credendum* almost necessarily obscured and even distorted the true character of faith; for belief in this dogma and belief in the sense which the apostles attach to the term, to assent to a dogma and to believe in Jesus Christ in such a way that this belief is inseparable from love—here are obviously two quite different things. But nevertheless the intellectualist misapprehension of the Church was not an absolutely inevitable consequence of this formal definition of the creed; for it was always open to the *Ecclesia* to interpret this credo in the sense of the primitive Christian apostolic *pisteuein*.

(c) Far more serious, however, was the erection of the third bulwark; that of the episcopal office. History shows how ill suited it was, in point of fact, for the purpose it was meant to serve. The replacement of the concept of tradition by that of legitimacy was bound to work itself out in all its fatal consequences; indeed, as we have already shown, it inevitably led to the fact that the fundamental and primitive testing of doctrine by Scripture ceased to operate. But not until much later did history make plain that the real effect of this bulwark had been actually to transform the innermost spirit of the thing it was desired to protect.

[1] See above, p. 33.

88

(ii) The second argument adduced to explain the necessity of creating the ecclesiastical office as a protective barrier runs as follows: the pneumatic-charismatic order which was typical of primitive Christianity was only possible as long as the *Ecclesia* was small. With the increase in the number of the faithful, with geographical expansion and the consequent manifold variety of circumstances and conditions, such a purely spiritual order became manifestly impossible. Fixed regulations, unambiguous relationships of superiority and subordination had to be made; the transition from a spiritual organism to an ecclesiastical organization was unavoidable.

We shall have to examine this argument in detail. But it is so closely connected with the third that it will be best to investigate both at the same time; we pass immediately therefore to the third reason which is usually alleged to justify the transformation of the *Ecclesia* into the Church:

(iii) With the non-appearance of the Parousia, with the continuance of the old order of things in so far as earthly life was concerned, the Christian community had to abandon its tense eschatological expectations: it had to reckon with the possibility of a long life for the *Ecclesia* and make its arrangements accordingly. With this change and inner relaxation, a decline in spiritual intensity was necessarily involved. The disappearance of the *pneuma* and of the order it had created inevitably made way for the substitution of a different kind of order—that of ecclesiastical administration.

At first sight these arguments seem in fact to be rather convincing. One cannot altogether deny them a certain amount of justification. But we must first of all draw attention to a fact which usually escapes notice. The decisive re-orientation of the *Ecclesia* in the direction of the Church does not in the least depend upon the above-mentioned factors, neither upon the militancy of the *Ecclesia* in the world, nor upon its numerical extension: it is rather of a purely inner, religious-theological nature. It depends in fact upon that primary shift of emphasis in the conception of what constitutes the means of salvation, as a result of which the meal, from being a corporate act of the community for its own strengthening and edification, became the real food of salvation and further-more, a mystic food which is distributed to the congregation by the priest. No external cause, neither gnostic heresy nor the numerical growth and spread of the Christian com-munion, had the slightest bearing upon this inward trans-formation. But it must be recognized, from the course of our previous discussion, that this change in the understanding of salvation, and its appointed means, led of necessity to that structural change in the community the effect of which was to produce the sacramental church of priesthood and laity. Not until afterwards were functions of authoritarian govern-ment assigned to the priest-bishop. And for the very same reason these functions possessed from the start a sacramental character. Because the episcopal ruler and bearer of auth-ority was a priestly person, therefore the order he instituted was a sacramental order—an order created and maintained by the apostolically *ordained* bishop. The quasi-legal adminis-tration of the Church—perhaps justified by its numerical extent—was a sacramental order, a rule of sacred canon law.

As far as the third argument is concerned, it confirms—negatively so to speak—our contention that church order is a substitute for the banished *pneuma*. The fact that the church began to fail in spiritual power is something which we may perhaps note, but which we cannot explain as a necessary consequence of increasing numbers. When we realize how considerably the Pauline mission had extended the Church already in the lifetime of the apostle, and reflect what enormous numbers had already to be catered for—at a time when Paul's genius had reached its zenith—in comparison, for example, with the membership of the first Christian com-munity at Jerusalem, then the equation of increasing num-bers and decreasing spiritual power becomes exceedingly doubtful. We could understand it if Paul, whose scope was so much vaster than the Jerusalem community had ever dared to dream, face to face with the latter had expressed himself thus: "I can no longer manage with your spiritual order, something more stable is required." We know, however, that the facts of history were clean contrary to this supposition.

It was Paul the world-missionary who in debate with the Jerusalem community represented the principle: no legalistic authoritarian government by the pillars of the Church, but government by Jesus, by His Word and His Spirit alone.

We have got to accept the decline in spiritual power simply as a fact, for which there is no explanation unless it be of a pastoral kind: life in the Spirit thus declines, just as "first love" cools.[1] Above all, the Johannine community, surpassing the Pauline in indifference to church order, shows us that the ebb of the Spirit's tide need have nothing whatsoever to do with receding expectations of the imminent return of the Christ. For precisely in Johannine circles, spirituality, mystical inspiration, reaches its peak and at the same time the expectation of the Parousia is clearly thrown into the background.

The truth is that in proportion as the Christian body ceases to be a spiritual unity, a *koinonia* in the primitive sense, the fine suppleness proper to a spiritual structure must give place to the coarser character of an organizational legalistic structure. It might well be the case, however, that incipient sacramentalism had more to do with the decline in spiritual vitality than had numerical growth. It is false to insist that the institutional development of the *Ecclesia* is a necessity involved in this numerical increase either directly or indirectly through the intermediate stage of diminishing spiritual inspiration.

But even supposing that the Church, in view of its extension and numerical growth, must have appreciated the necessity of creating an administrative juridical organization: why was it inevitable that this organization should bear a holy sacramental character? Admitting that the possession of the Spirit was no longer sufficiently assured to maintain the order and unity of the Christian society, who gave this Society the right to transfer the character of the holy, the pneumatic, precisely to that element of legalistic administration, the introduction of which now appeared to be a regrettable necessity? What sort of justification was there for this

[1] Rev. 2:4.

particular *quid pro quo*, namely, that the secular element—
the juridical organization—should be presented under a
spiritual guise? that the hybrid monster—"sacred ecclesiastical polity"—should be created? Granted, the temptation to
do so was very pressing. For hitherto it had been the Holy
Ghost who had been the author of unity and coherence in
the community. Hence it was tempting to try to pass off as
holy and spiritual the juridical polity which now, after the
real or supposed failure of a spiritual order, seemed essential.
Such a temptation was all the more powerful because a similar change had already been effected in regard to the sacrament, in that a sacral thing, a material means of salvation, a
pharmakon tes athanasias had been created. Hence the origin
of a *sacred* ecclesiastical polity is also to be sought for in
sacramentalism and nowhere else.

It was, of course, as we have already seen, the person of the
episcopal ruler, now a priest, upon whom the administrative
authoritarian functioning of the church as it were devolved.
And it was too the sacrament of Holy Orders, ordination,
which made possible this ascription of a sacred character to
ecclesiastical polity.

The assertion that the development of the *Ecclesia* into the
Church was a necessity is thus by no means incontrovertible.
It may be challenged on various grounds. It does not stand
the test of closer inspection, however much it may contain
elements of truth.

What is the result of this "development" which is virtually
a transformation, a fundamental change of character? The
community of Jesus Christ is henceforth identical with an
organization, an institution, a holy thing. Henceforth the
Church cannot be mentioned or thought of without the
implication of this constitutional element. The *Ecclesia* is no
longer conceivable without the bishop; now for the first time
community and bishop combine to constitute the Church.
Accordingly, in talking of the Church, one or the other of
these constituent parts is predominant, but its later development, without any shadow of a doubt, proceeds in such a way
that the Church now understands itself to be an institution,

resting upon the priestly office. This process began with the vindication of the inviolable sacred rights and privileges of presbyters or bishops in the first epistle of Clement, and almost at the same time we find Ignatius writing about the monarchical episcopate, the bishop who as the vicar of Christ fashions and secures the unity of the Christian society (2). And now the process goes steadily further, to be sure with a kind of inevitability and inner logic: though not of course with an absolute irresistible determinism. For the small stages by which the development in this direction gradually proceeds are not completed without opposition (3). But the inner logic of the movement is stronger than any opposition, until indeed a point is reached at which a powerful cleavage develops—though without convulsive strife—the eastern half of the Church remaining stationary and only the western half going further on its self-chosen path. Then finally some centuries later the development, or rather the transformation, has gone so far that fundamental opposition becomes inevitable, attacking the movement at its roots, while on the other hand the forces which are determined upon this transformation are thereby incited to complete it all the more quickly by the erection of a system of church polity in which sacramentalism and institutionalism have brought each other to a climax of perfection, a culminating point beyond which no further development is conceivable.

Chapter Ten

THE CHRIST-COMMUNITY AND THE CHURCHES OF HISTORY

The church of the papacy developed, by a long process of transformation, out of the original Christian society, the *Ecclesia* of the New Testament. This process of transformation begins already at the close of the apostolic age. The early catholic church, the first result of it, remained unconscious of such a remoulding process. But in the course of history that continuous development, whose final term is the Roman Catholic church, suffered a series of interruptions from which arose non-Roman churches of various kinds. These can be divided principally into two main groups: those which appeared before and those which appeared after the decisive change from early to neo-catholicism.

The first break—apart from small secessions without any real significance for the present situation (1) is formed by the separation of the eastern from the western church and the Greek Orthodox church which sprang from it. In 858 we have the schism of Photius; in 1054 the final cleavage between the Latin and the Greek forms of Christianity. Since this separation took place in the early Middle Ages, well before the crisis of the Reformation, the Greek Orthodox may be regarded as that church which clung to and preserved the stage of ecclesiastical development which at that moment had been reached. In essence it is the early catholic church, the one therefore which affirms the measure of "development" that had taken place before the critical transition to the neo-catholic Roman papacy and considers that development to be simply a process of unfolding or flowering, not one of re-fashioning or transformation. As such it is the living historical proof of the fact that the logical further development to its final term of the process by which the New Testament *Ecclesia* became ultimately a complete sacramental institution, was by no means inevitable. The early catholic, Greek Orthodox church has shown convincingly its power to live; for the following nine centuries it has been able to remain at the stage of ecclesiasticism reached in the eleventh century, and in that ecclesiastical framework it has been capable of imparting the Gospel to the peoples of Eastern Europe and of deeply influencing their life by the Gospel so understood. All the attempts of Rome to cancel this schism have so far failed; the Greek Orthodox church is thoroughly aware of the deep-seated differences which separate it from the Roman church, fashioned as it is by the totalitarianism of the papacy, and, in the face of the latter, passionately asserts its claim to be the true Catholic Church. From a strictly historical point of view we must thoroughly endorse the claim of Greek Orthodoxy that it arose not from a revolutionary movement, but on the contrary from its undeviating loyalty to tradition, whilst the Roman church has diverged from traditional catholicism by a revolutionary process. Indeed we might go even further and add this: if the Roman church likewise had remained at the stage of ecclesiastical development which had been reached at the time of this separation, then probably the second schism, so much more radical than the first—the secession of the Reformed churches—would never have happened, at least not on the scale on which it did happen, due to the fact that in the meantime the western church had become the neo-catholic Roman papal church. For this reason, in spite of all far-reaching differences, conversation, even mutual understanding and co-operation remain possible between the early catholic, Greek Orthodox church and the churches which emerged from the Reformation.

In the west, however, the further development from the early catholic to the neo-catholic, Roman, papal church did actually occur. The Greek catholic church is not wrong in regarding this further development as a process of revolutionary transformation. That is what in fact it is. But at the same time the eastern church forgets that this new development in western Christendom constituted hardly a greater transformation than the one by which, in the course of the first 1,000 years, the *Ecclesia* of the New Testament had become the early catholic church itself. The distance from the early catholic church of the year 1000 to the neo-catholic Roman church of 1870 or 1918 is not greater, measured by the standard of New Testament Christianity, than the distance which separates the primitive Christian community from the early catholic church of the year 1000. Further, it does not realize that this new development, which proceeded apace from the middle of the twelfth century onwards, in spite of its revolutionary appearance was nothing but the consistent following to its termination of the path which had been struck out with the first epistle of Clement and the letters of Ignatius. Looking back, we may and indeed must say without hesitation that the eastern church stopped half-way on the road which led from the New Testament *Ecclesia* to the papal church of the present day.

With this second stage, the transition to the neo-catholic, Roman, papacy, the alienation of the historical Church from the New Testament *Ecclesia* attained such proportions that a radical movement of protest in the sense of a return to the origins of Christianity became inevitable. The Reformation took place, first that of Luther, then that of Calvin—which in essentials had begun with Zwingli at the same time as Luther's movement—and from these two streams arose distinctive types of churches which up to the present day preach the Christian Gospel in powerful and creative forms and mould the lives of their members in accordance with their understanding of the Christ. The principle which underlies these new ecclesiastical formations is the determination to go back to and renew the original life of Christianity—*reformatio* —hence the determination to revive the *Ecclesia* of the New Testament. But this powerful impulse to restore what is lost was capable of various interpretations, and from this manifold variety of interpretation had proceeded the diversity of the post-Reformation churches and of those structures which are called sects by the churches and which regard themselves as congregations or fellowships. In a certain sense the Lutheran church forms a class apart, while the Calvinistic churches and the sects belong together (2).

Luther's protest was directed against the holy institution as such, against the understanding of the community of Christ as a Church. Fundamentally he wanted to undo the ecclesiastical development of the *Ecclesia* (3). Therefore he started at the vitally significant point: that of sacred canon law. The decisive act of Luther's reformation was the burning of the *Corpus juris canonici* (December 10, 1520). This rejection of sacramental canon law was the inevitable consequence of his conception of faith and salvation as a being justified in Christ. But the organization in practice of his Christian community required as an absolute necessity both the co-operation of the state and the use of a legal administration (4). Luther allowed the territorial princes to organize the church and to govern it by law; but—and here Luther remained faithful to his vision of the *Ecclesia*—this legal administration is, in his opinion, a purely worldly matter, not sacred: it has nothing whatever to do with salvation as such. Even the office, now conceived on administrative lines—and even the bishop's office—is no priestly function and has no sacramental meaning; it is a purely secular juridical institution, necessary for the organization of the Christian community, but quite irrelevant to the faith of the individual (5).

Not so Calvin. He is concerned with the return to the New Testament *Ecclesia* not only from the standpoint of the individual's faith, but likewise from the standpoint of church order. Hence for Calvin there exists a sacred New Testament church polity, which can and must be reproduced just as one can and must revive the New Testament conception of Christian faith. In that Calvin recognizes the existence of a sacred church polity—the one presumably contained in the New Testament—he stands nearer than Luther to early catholicism, just as he has a far closer, more positive relationship to the early Church Fathers in general than is the case with the Wittenberg reformer.

There results, however, from this very principle of the possible and necessary reproduction of the New Testament *Ecclesia* in its formal structure, the continued process of unceasing church reformations: for the so-called "sectarian"

G   97

developments of those times were at bottom nothing but a protest against the insufficient radicalism with which the New Testament *Ecclesia* had been restored, the attempt to take more seriously the *imitatio ecclesiae* than the established churches had done—whether of the Lutheran or Zwinglian-Calvinistic variety. The never-ending fissure of new sects from the Church springs ever afresh from the impulse to approximate more closely to the *Ecclesia* of the New Testament, indeed to become completely identical with it in every particular. In these attempts the salient feature was discovered now here, now there, so that there arose not only a great number but also a great variety of ecclesiastical structures, each one of which claimed and still claims to be the most faithful copy of the original.

Yet the closest possible approximation to the New Testament *Ecclesia* has not been the sole driving force behind church movements in recent times; a reformation of quite a different character and origin has taken place at the same time as modern sectarian developments: namely, the Anglo-Catholic revival of early catholicism (6). This revival could take as its starting-point the fact that the Anglican Church which resulted from the Reformation had institutionally, but not theologically, a very different character from the churches of the continental European Reformation; since, while it made a decisive breach with the papacy, it retained its traditional hierarchical structure. Therefore without making any changes in the ecclesiastical polity as such, the Anglo-Catholic movement of the nineteenth century could content itself merely with modifying the theological interpretation of the existing hierarchical church by assimilating it to the spirit of early catholicism. The result was that in so far as this new interpretation penetrated, there arose now in the west also "an early catholic church" of great significance similar to the Greek Orthodox church in the account it gave of itself. The fact that also a continental early catholic church emerged from the repudiation by a number of Roman Catholic bishops of the claims of the Vatican need only be just mentioned here, for no major significance can be assigned to this tiny split-off church, in spite of its spiritual vitality.

So then we are confronted by the fact not only of a multiplicity but also of a great variety of churches. In more recent times, to be sure, the impulse of the *imitatio ecclesiae* has been overshadowed by the appearance of a motive which has had a contrary effect—the thought, namely, that the mere fact of the multiplicity and diversity of the Christian churches stands in contradiction to the New Testament *Ecclesia*. If you take seriously the thought of the Body of Christ, it follows as a necessary consequence that there cannot be more than one Church. Hence it is maintained by some that the most urgently necessary of all ecclesiastical reforms is a return to the unity of the primitive church. But with this religious-theological impulse there was combined a much more powerful dynamic one, namely, the realization of the relative weakness of a divided Christian Church, and the desire by the recovery of unity to remove the obvious scandal of division and to win for the Church a new influence upon the life of the world. Such a combination of motives has given birth to the strongest church movement of modern times, that is, the ecumenical movement, which already can count a number of very significant practical results to its credit, among which the most important are the World Council of Churches which was formed in 1947, the reunion of the Churches of South India, and the National Council of the Protestant Churches of America.

Thus now we stand faced by our own particular problem. In view of this whole complex of ecclesiastical matters, what theological interpretation are we to give of the Church? What is the Church, and, as our fundamental presupposition, recognizing the Word of Scripture to be the final and absolute norm (7) what is the true Church and its proper task?

First of all, we must note an objective fact: all these various churches—the Roman Catholic as much as the Quakers—claim to be the true Church in the New Testament sense. Each of them, though in a different way, appeals to the New Testament and finds therein the justification for its own special characteristics. What are we to say of all these claims

99

and counter-claims, each of which, interpreted literally, is irreconcilable with the others? From the point of view of the New Testament which is the true Church? In answer to this question it follows from all that we have hitherto said that the very idea of "the true Church" is self-contradictory (8) so long as we regard the New Testament as the criterion of the truth. For the conclusion to be drawn from the New Testament is that just this ecclesiastical development of the community of Jesus, of the *Ecclesia*, involves a change of essence, a transformation standing in contradiction to New Testament truth. This is especially clear from the fact that the Roman church, where this transforming process has been carried to its logical conclusion, regards itself as the only Church and of course as the one and only true Church. Precisely those factors which make it the most ecclesiastical of all churches make it necessarily the most exclusive also. If the "true Church" is the one which develops the ecclesiastical element to its utmost pitch of perfection, then the Roman church is not only the most perfect, but may also maintain that it is the only true Church. Negatively it results from the same considerations that in proportion as its ecclesiastical nature is essential to any church, it has a correspondingly great share in that process of alienation from the primitive *Ecclesia* which with the Roman church reaches its maximum.

What are we to say now of these claims of the various churches—even of those who repudiate the title of "church" —to be the true Church, the *Ecclesia* of the New Testament?

We begin with the greatest (measured by worldly standards) and even yet the most powerful—the Roman church. It claims to be historically the oldest, since it has developed in unbroken continuity from the *Ecclesia* of apostolic times. In making these assertions, it forgets that it has a rival who with the very best right can dispute its pretensions—namely, the Greek Orthodox church; it is incontestable that this church too has grown uninterruptedly out of the primitive church of apostolic times; that it has become separated from Rome means simply, of course, from its own point of view, that Rome has become separated from it. Nor would this be the only criticism; it could go further and say that the Roman church after its secession has undergone a transformation which signifies nothing less than a decisive break with early Catholic traditions. Church historians can scarcely object to this thesis; they would rather have much to say in its support. The primacy of the Roman Pope has never been admitted by the eastern church in the sense which Rome intends, much less still in the sense which Rome only developed and defined after the separation. For this sense constitutes a new departure (9). The Roman theologians will not fail indeed to derive this new departure from the Lord's words to Peter, and thus to represent the history of the Papacy as a process of organic unfolding. (10)

For the churches of the west, however, the situation is somewhat different. They cannot deny that they all stand, as it were, on the shoulders of the Roman church; from a purely historical point of view, the Reformation and post-Reformation churches too are neither possible nor conceivable without the 1,500 years of western church history which preceded the Reformation and which was, in great part, a history of the Roman church. The reformers themselves were, of course, baptized Roman Catholics before they became reformers. And the churches which they founded—together with their derivatives—owe to this great church, which existed before them, the Bible and the whole Christian tradition without which none of them could have lived or would ever have come into existence. The Reformation was a cleansing of the church but not a totally new beginning. The historical continuity of the years 30 to 1500 is the very foundation of the life of the reformed churches also. Therefore it is impossible, without cutting oneself off from one's roots, to judge the Roman church in its negative aspects only, however anti-Romish one may be. But apart from this evident historical fact, who could really deny that the Roman church too lives in the power of the Gospel of Jesus Christ? that in it too, in spite of all transmutations, elements of the primitive Christian *Ecclesia* still exist and make themselves felt? that it is still a home of genuine faith in Christ and of much Christian and brotherly love? indeed may we Pro-. testants, who perceive so clearly the gulf between the mighty ecclesiastical structure of Rome and the *Ecclesia* of the New Testament, deny that in the Roman as in other catholic churches, elements of that *Ecclesia* have remained alive which in the far too sweeping reactions of the Reformation and post-Reformation epochs were unfortunately thrust aside? However vast the abyss which divides Rome from the primitive church, however unfounded its pretension to be the true and the only true Church—to refuse it all connection with the apostolic *Ecclesia* would exceed the just measure of Reformation criticism.

But the reformers had received as the most precious deposit of tradition from the hands of the Roman church—which of course was the sole church existing in the west before them— the Bible and the primitive tradition, and they used this primitive tradition as the canon into which it had crystallized: they used it as the norm for the criticism of the contemporary church. The Reformation arose out of such critical testing and out of the new appreciation of faith which had been gained from contact with the text of Holy Scripture. The primitive tradition became the means of cleansing that which had resulted from historical development: had the Roman church allowed herself to be thus purified, it is hardly conceivable that a break could have occurred. Continuity was destroyed not by the Reformation itself but by the im- penitence of the papal church which obstinately refused to adopt the measure of renewal and cleansing entailed by this legitimate degree of criticism. Luther never left the catholic church, but was thrown out of it by the Pope. The separation took place through the action of the Pope, not through that of the reformer. That fact too must be kept in mind when one speaks of the importance of unbroken tradition!

Did the Reformation in fact restore the *Ecclesia* of apostolic times? The lasting merit of the reformers was to have recog- nized, as had never been done before or since, the great im- portance of the Word of Jesus Christ as the source of life of the Christian community. The contribution which they thus made to the world, and to the Roman and all other catholic churches, is of immeasurable value. For this ultimate and decisive importance of the Word had been forgotten—and not only in the Roman church but previously also in the early catholic church. The reformers therefore framed their conception of the Church exclusively with reference to the Word of Christ and therewith took a powerful stride across the centuries to the first Christian community of the apostolic age. But to go on to claim that the Lutheran or Calvinistic church is identical with the *Ecclesia* of the apostles, will not do. They are so much the less close to it in proportion as they emphasize their ecclesiastical character. For where in these Reformation churches is that oneness of communion with Christ and communion with the brethren in which precisely the paradoxical existence of the Church consists? The Lutheran or rather Melanchthonian definition of the Church: *est autem Ecclesia congregatio sanctorum in qua evangelium recte docetur et recte administrantur sacramenta,* contains of course decisive insights into the essential nature of the *Ecclesia;* but no one will suppose that one of the apostles would recognize again in this formula the *Ecclesia* of which he had had living experience.

Calvin's great merit in the history of the Church is to have been able to carry through the Reformation in such wise that out of it arose—of course, not without some important state co-operation—essentially autonomous churches, independent of the state, standing foursquare on their own feet. Through his genius for the organization of the church he rescued the Reformation and made it possible for the reformed churches to weather the tremendous storm of the Counter-Reformation. The Protestant world of the west has been much more strongly marked by the imprint of Calvin than by that of Luther. In spite of all this, any one who is determined to lend an unprejudiced ear to the witness of the New Testament Christian community must recognize as unfounded Calvin's claim to have revived the primitive Christian *Ecclesia.* Certainly Calvin (though not Luther) far excelled Melanchthon and Lutheran orthodoxy in that he gave much greater scope to the element of fellowship, and laid greater weight upon the inseparability of faith and love, than could ever be the case in Lutheranism where everything culminates in the right confession and the right way of believing. But that the form of government which he gave to the Genevan church and taught dogmatically as the correct ecclesiastical polity, was in reality that of the New Testament—this was an exegetical error and in point of fact implied a return to the mentality which had given birth to sacrosanct canon law. His equations: Pastors=the apostles, doctors=the prophets, presbytery= the *presbyterai*, and deacons=the *diakonoi* of the New Testament are completely impossible exegetically, but from a practical point of view of the highest importance as approximations to the living realities of the New Testament *Ecclesia*.

The position is not essentially different, either positively or negatively, with regard to the so-called sects or societies which arose as struggles in the wake of the Reformation. They all sprang from the desire to get nearer to the New Testament *Ecclesia* than the great reformed churches had done, which they accused, and with some justification, of having insufficiently cleansed the Roman leaven. They reproached these churches above all with having failed to sever the age-long sinister association of church and state and so with having taken over from Rome the Constantinian-Theodosian inheritance. They on the contrary wished to form themselves into societies of true believers, free from the fetters of the state, after the manner of the primitive Christian community. They rejected the fundamental principle *cujus regio ejus religio* and therewith maintenance by the state (11). But they too fell into the easily understandable error of Calvin; they thought they could discover in the *Ecclesia* of the New Testament a form of administration, a sacred polity, which might be reproduced by the closest possible imitation; at the same time, however, they all constituted themselves on a basis of civil law, like that of any worldly society. Thus they believed in their fashion in a sacrosanct church order discoverable in the New Testament, and they attempted to combine this with purely secular law. At the same time it ought not to be disputed that many of the characteristics which marked the New Testament *Ecclesia* have left upon them a clearer and stronger impress than upon the Reformation churches. In particular it is the element of fellowship, brotherhood, and correspondingly the close relationship between Christian faith and the practical realities of daily life, which is the peculiar property of these "sects" as opposed to all orthodox "churches" and which to-day, more than ever, when men are hungering and thirsting after fellowship as never before, gives them their immensely powerful attractiveness. To compare extremes: In *this* particular respect, the "Society of Friends", the Quakers, stands incomparably nearer to the *Ecclesia* than does the Church of Rome. On the other hand, even Rome, but more especially the non-Roman catholic churches, precisely through their emphasis upon the sacraments and the liturgy, have retained from the primitive *Ecclesia* elements of decisive importance which the Quakers have almost completely let slip.

As the final result of our critical-historical investigation we must draw the conclusion that none of the existing churches or sects may justifiably claim to be the *Ecclesia* of apostolic times, while on the other hand none of them is without certain elements essential to the *Ecclesia* which are lacking in others. That moment stressed by the Greek Orthodox and Roman churches, namely, unbroken historical continuity from the apostolic age, is undoubtedly a powerful and living reality; but it is counterbalanced by the fact that this continuity is at the same time a transformation, whose final term has but little similarity with the starting-point. The churches of the Reformation can claim that in their doctrine they come nearest to New Testament Christianity and that this doctrine is of decisive importance; but pure doctrine—quite apart from the fact that when ossified into a system of orthodoxy it ceases to be New Testament in spirit—is, if divorced from the warm realities of church fellowship and brotherhood in Christ, only an element of the *Ecclesia*, not the latter itself. Similarly, all the essays of post-Reformation sects suffer from the misconception that the *Ecclesia* of the New Testament is in essence imitable.

Chapter Eleven

THE TASK BEFORE THE CHURCHES—TO SERVE THE GROWTH
OF THE "ECCLESIA"

What we know as the church or churches resulting
from historical developments cannot claim to be
the *Ecclesia* in the New Testament sense. Some of
these churches—the Greek Orthodox and the Roman Catholic—in comparison with those which have arisen out of and
since the Reformation, enjoy the great advantage that they
have become what they are and have not been made. Through
a long and continuous process of evolution they have developed into what we see them to-day. By contrast with other
churches, they can appeal to the principle that the *Ecclesia*
cannot be made, that something which was made by an act
of men cannot be the *Ecclesia*. This process, however,
through which they have become what they are, is not merely
(as they suppose) a process of unfolding, of the organic
development of something originally given, albeit only in
embryonic form, but is at the same time a process of transformation and change whose final product is a Church which
—as is especially the case with the Roman church—can
hardly any longer be identified with its prototype but on the
contrary conflicts with the essential nature of the *Ecclesia*.

The churches of the Reformation on the other hand can
claim for themselves that they have sprung from the determination to stop the process by which the essence of the
Church was being subtly transformed, from the desire for a
reformatio after the pattern of the original *Ecclesia*. But they
cannot deny that they have been fabricated by a human act,
whether it be the foundation-act of a state friendly to the
Reformation—as for example the churches of Germany,
Switzerland, England, Scotland and Holland—or whether it
be the foundation-act of individual Christians who united
for the purpose of creating a new, truly reformed church or

society. But the New Testament *Ecclesia* did not spring into existence thus. It stands out as something essentially other, both by contrast with those Catholic churches which have resulted from the process of transformation, as also by contrast with the Protestant churches which were made by a foundation-act either of the state or of private individuals. The most palpable sign of this characteristic difference lies in the matter of organization and polity. All the churches known to history are quasi-political structures, institutions in a legal sense. The fundamental thesis of Rudolph Sohm, that the essential nature of the Church (he means the *Ecclesia*) stands in antithesis to all law, is indisputable whether, as in the Catholic churches, this law is conceived as sacred or whether, as in the Reformed churches, it is interpreted on secular lines; whether, as in the churches founded by the great reformers themselves, it is a public, or whether, as in the free churches and sects, it is a private type of polity. In this legalistic, semi-political nature of the churches, their character as institutions appears most prominently, and it is precisely this factor which distinguishes them most sharply from the *Ecclesia* of the New Testament and divides them from it by an impassable gulf. The juridical institutional character of the historical churches reveals the fact that they are either the product of a process of transformation, or that they were established by human agency, as for example the reformed church of Zürich was set up by the decree of the Zürich council.

The *Ecclesia*, however, was never thus inaugurated and cannot be inaugurated, just as the *Ecclesia* knows nothing whatever of a sacred polity. It is no institution. Therefore a church can never *be* the *Ecclesia* either by purification or re-creation. The task before the churches cannot be that of becoming the *Ecclesia*—this would be an utter impossibility —but only that of furthering the growth of the *Ecclesia* or at least—and this is by no means a minimum which goes without saying—not hindering it. In all this the meaning of the *Ecclesia* is what we recognized from the New Testament as its characteristic essence: communion with God through Jesus

Christ, and rooted in this and springing from it, communion or brotherhood with man. The oneness of communion with Christ and communion with man is the characteristic mark of the *Ecclesia*. In this a second characteristic is implied: the oneness of the religious community—religion being here understood in the usual, cultic sense of divine worship—with the individual church members' religious sacramental approach to everyday workaday realities. In the New Testament the symbol and sign of this twofold unity was precisely that which later became the pre-eminently cultic, the "sacrament"—that is, the fellowship of the meal.

This communion with Christ and fellowship with man is above all anchored in the Word of Christ which testifies to the action and gift of God, in particular to the atonement through the Cross and to the heavenly inheritance of eternal life. This Word claims the loyalty of the hearers, their loyalty to the sovereign will of God, and to His fatherly grace. But it is not to be identified with the theology derived from it; it is rather the gift of the Holy Ghost, creating life and obedience. It is therefore inseparable from the witness of the new creation in Christ, and never to be divorced from the living realities of communion with Christ and fellowship with man.

Communion with Christ is therefore deeply grounded not only in the Word but also in the effectual working of the Holy Ghost as of a super-logical power which even without words can prove its reality through the testimony of love, of the inward peace proper to those who are reconciled through the Cross, of their unfailing joy in the midst of sorrow, through the power which knits the brethren into a unity, through their ready sympathy with the distresses and needs of others, through their willingness to make personal sacrifices understood as a self-explanatory consequence flowing from the sacrifice of Christ. The spirit animating the community proves its holiness in that it ever seeks the honour of God and declares all that the members of the *Ecclesia* have, are, and are capable of doing, to be the gift of God in Jesus Christ.

Where Jesus Christ is thus present among men, there the *Ecclesia* exists dynamically. Not an invisible church! For this fellowship in Christ is not merely an object of faith, but is at the same time a palpable living reality of experience visible to faith. Indeed something of it is even visible to unbelievers —by love "will all men know that ye are my disciples". "See how they love one another" is the testimony of the heathen, while of course the ground and the ultimate depths of this love is neither known nor recognizable to the unbelieving world, namely, the presence of the Head of this Body which the faithful may indeed perceive with the eye of faith but never with their physical vision.

Because and in so far as it is always and only a question of the *Ecclesia* in its dynamic empirical existence, the setting up of dogmatic as of ethical and social criteria can have only a relative, even ambiguous, value: for who can establish criteria to judge whether or not the Holy Ghost is really active in a human heart to which God is only just beginning to reveal Himself? Who would wish to propose criteria of membership which in certain circumstances would exclude precisely those whom God in secret has begun to draw unto Himself? The boundaries of the Church face to face with the world must therefore remain invisible to the eyes of men; a full dogmatic confession can deceive just as much as the entire absence of any such a thing.

To this *Ecclesia* which is always thus a dynamic reality and nothing more, the existing churchly institutions are related as means—*externa subsidia*—in very diverse ways and proportions: but even the greatest alienation from the New Testament *Ecclesia*, the most obvious change from the essence of the *Ecclesia* into that of the Church, need not absolutely preclude the latter from becoming an instrument for the growth and renewal of the former.

As a convinced Protestant I do not doubt that God can use even the means of the papal Mass—which our fathers not without good reason called an "accursed idolatry"[1]—to bring men into communion with the Lord Jesus Christ and to open their hearts to the needs of the brethren, just as I am certain that such communion with Christ and fellowship

[1] Heidelberg Catechism Fr. 80.

with man are to be found among the Quakers who know no sacraments, who yet all the more—more in fact than most churches—lay stress upon the working of brotherly love as the very expression of true belief. It is a relatively simple matter to compare the received orthodox teaching of any one church with the teachings of the New Testament; were this the final criterion, the nearness or remoteness of a given church from the New Testament *Ecclesia* would be soon decided: but of what use is the best officially declared teaching if it shows that it is powerless to make the members of that church living followers of Jesus and that church itself a living fellowship with Him?

From the standpoint which we have now reached, we must give up not only the attempt to find a *vera Ecclesia* as such, but even that of measuring the individual churches by any such supposed criterion. On the one hand, we shall be open to the significance of the historical continuity of the catholic churches and to what, in virtue of their stable structure, they have accomplished throughout the centuries in preserving the Gospel tradition; on the other hand we shall with equal candour take into account what ecclesiastically irregular and undeveloped societies have done for the propagation of the Name of Christ and the formation of a living communion in Him throughout the whole world. The idea of the church which has resulted from the course of history has had among other consequences the fact that when the true church is sought, it is easy to overlook certain forms of Christian fellowship which lack indeed specifically ecclesiastical features, but which have developed all the more manifestly momentous aspects of the *Ecclesia*.

We must reckon with the fact that in modern times—for reasons which we need not go into now—new organizations for the spread of the Gospel and the realization of fellowship in Christ have been and are being developed. These organizations are far removed from what had hitherto been understood by the term Church, but just for that reason offer more useful means for the fulfilment of the one aim that matters than the majority of the churches. Since for the most part they have arisen out of very practical necessities and are inspired by a particularly lively sense of fellowship and brotherhood—so often lacking in the churches—they have not seldom, in spite of the fact that they are not churches and do not set out to be, more in common with the *Ecclesia* of the New Testament than have our classical churches themselves or even the so-called sects of the post-Reformation period. We are thinking of course of such things as the Home Mission of Wichern in Germany, of the World Alliance of Y.M.C.A.'s, of the Student Christian Movement, of the Oxford Group Movement (now M.R.A.) or even of missionary societies such as the Basle or China Inland Missions, none of which has an organic connection with any church. How many millions have here (rather than in any of the churches) learnt to know Christ and to experience fellowship with others in and through Him, have here found their spiritual and Christian home, which they have bitterly missed when later perhaps they joined some church (1).

It is becoming increasingly clear that the churches, from the point of view of continuity of doctrine and preaching, are still indispensable and indeed far superior to every other type of organization, but it is equally clear that as regards winning souls and creating live cells of Christian fellowship they stand far behind other and more recent formations and in the future will probably be cast into the shade by the latter. They have long since lost the monopoly of preaching Christ and still more that of creating Christian fellowship. As already in the post-Reformation period the distinction between church and sect became meaningless—unless it be that sect was defined in the sense of heresy rather than that of schism—so in more recent times the idea of the church in the hitherto accepted sense of the term has been becoming more and more problematical, and practically a hindrance in the performance of the very work for which the churches exist. It is clear from the course of the historical process itself that the church is a historically developed form of the *Ecclesia* and therefore subject to the relativity that conditions all history.

From this point of view the so-called ecumenical problem

presents itself likewise in a new light. It cannot be denied that the division of the Christian communion into a multiplicity of single churches stands in contradiction to the very nature of the *Ecclesia* as the Body of Christ and presents one of the greatest obstacles to the understanding of the Christian message—a mischief which it must be the endeavour of all Christians to remove. From this follows of necessity the ecumenical task. But it would be jumping to conclusions to suppose that the aim of the ecumenical movement must be ecclesiastical reunion, the organizational union of the various historically developed churches. Certain as is the fact that a number of competing churches represents a scandal, equally certain is it on the other hand that a variety of forms of Christian fellowship is a necessity. As God in former times spoke in divers manners[1] so to-day He wills to attract in various ways men of manifold temperaments. One to whom a high church liturgical service brings the highest measure of spiritual good is obviously a very different type of man from the one to whom a Salvation Army gathering with hand-clapping and trombones does the same spiritual service. Should not the Lord be able to be in the midst of them in both cases? Diversity of liturgical and other forms by no means precludes unity in Christ. But on the other hand to emphasize the need for reunion of the quasi-political church bodies implies an over-valuation of the church as an institution and therefore favours clericalism, the false identification of church and *Ecclesia*. Furthermore it is of course usually the case when it comes to such reunions that the more ecclesiastical, that is the clerical side, is the victor; and the less churchly, the less clerical, is the vanquished (2). It would point to the conclusion that in the last resort such a movement must end with the victory of the most ecclesiastical church—the Roman.

Far more important than this organizational reunion of the historical churches is the readiness of individual Christians, and also especially of church officials, to co-operate in a spirit of brotherliness. In proportion as the insight here

[1] Heb. 1:1.

expressed gains ground—that none of the churches is the New Testament *Ecclesia*—then the most important obstcale to this work of co-operation in mutual regard is overcome. Confessionalism, the isolationist tendency hostile to co-operation, arises precisely from the false opinion that a particular church is the true *Ecclesia*, the legitimate heir of the Christian fellowship of the New Testament. This confessionalism, often grounded in and nourished by the deepest faith, can only be overcome by taking its fundamental intention—to be guided by the *Ecclesia* of the New Testament—more seriously than it does itself and by not referring ecumenical aims to motives which are of a worldly rather than a spiritual character. Once it is recognized that, regarded from the point of view of the New Testament and the apostolic *Ecclesia*, the historical Church must be considered to be the product of a transforming process, then true churchliness is attained and false churchliness overcome. No true *Ecclesia* can be made out of twenty ecclesiastical institutions; Christian fellowship can spring only from spiritual knowledge of Christ, which implies the will to brotherhood in Christ. For in Christ recognition of the truth and the will to fellowship with man are one. Only faith which proves its reality by love is true faith.

This vision of things is alive in many parts of Christendom, but almost everywhere is impeded, to some extent even made ineffective, by a false ecclesiastical ideal. The latter stems from a wrong understanding of the *Ecclesia* as a church: once this misunderstanding is removed, a powerful step has been taken towards overcoming the divisions of the churches.

It is unmistakable that to-day, in Europe especially, there prevails a far-reaching mistrust of everything that has to do with the Church even among such as are quite open to the Gospel of Jesus Christ. We must not forget that the idea of the Church is heavily compromised by nineteen hundred years of Church history, and that the churches have accumulated obstacles between Jesus Christ and the individual man which are often impossible to surmount. The suspicion of all that goes by the name of the Church is therefore most certainly not to be referred exclusively to a false individualism, but on the contrary flows not least from the recognition that that fellowship which is the theme of the Gospel of Jesus and the Apostles, not only is missing from the churches but quite often is simply not desired there. For who thinks, when he hears the word "church", of brotherhood, of a vital creative togetherness?

On the other hand, the Roman church—the most ecclesiastical of all—has for many a great attraction at the present time just because it corresponds to the contemporary tendency towards collectivism. This fact is more than suspicious. Contemporary man, who fears the anarchy into which a rationalistic and individualistic philosophy of enlightenment has led the world, is anxious to seize what appears to be the antithesis of anarchy—totalitarian collectivism whether it be in the profane atheistic form of communism, or in the sacral-sacramental form of the papal church. In both cases a security is offered him which relieves him of ultimate personal responsibility. He misunderstands his own deepest longing for fellowship and seeks to appease it by something which bears only a seeming resemblance to fellowship—namely, collectivist unity.

The *Ecclesia* of the New Testament is the true but extremely paradoxical antithesis to both individualistic anarchy and totalitarian collectivism. To belong to the *Ecclesia* means both to be committed to the highest personal responsibility and to renounce all merely private isolated individual existence. Faith in Jesus Christ is at one and the same time freedom and obligation and both in the highest degree. Only he is free who is reconciled with God, with himself and with his fellows; only he is free who is utterly dependent upon God; and whosoever is "free indeed"[1] through the Son who makes him dependent upon the Father, is entirely committed and entirely bound up with the life of his fellows. He is bound by the obligations of the situation in which he finds himself, and it is this constraint which makes him a real person; through it, his life is bound up firstly with those who share with him that deepest inner obligation and then also with all those who

[1] John 8:36.

114

have been created for the same God and for whose sakes the atoning death of Christ has taken place. For Jesus Christ died for the world and not merely for believers; He made atonement for all mankind, and not for believers only. Therefore he who belongs to Him knows also that he owes all men the service of truth and love.

This freedom and this obligation are of the essence of the Gospel of Jesus Christ and the New Testament *Ecclesia*. But what is called the Church in history allows you to see so little, so pathetically little of this freedom which is bondage and this bondage which is freedom. That is the reason why on the one hand so many, although they have learned precisely this lesson from the Gospel, refuse to have anything to do with the Church, and why on the other hand many are driven by their collectivist instincts into the arms of that church which has made the institution a substitute for fellowship. We have therefore to fear a false churchliness just as much as a false individualism. The false churchliness springs from the misunderstanding of the *Ecclesia Christi* as an institution. This misunderstanding which in recent times has so often lurked behind the slogan "Let the Church be the Church" is the most effective hindrance to the growth of the true *Ecclesia* in the so-called churches, and to the mutual understanding and co-operation of Christians which is so distressingly absent. It is not an organized unity of the churches that we most need; on the contrary, such a thing could in the last resort merely serve to increase the fundamental evil—the misunderstanding of the Church—by identifying, once more, Church and institution. What we need is the Holy Ghost who is promised to faith in Jesus Christ and who, where He is powerfully operative, brings about that freedom in obligation and that sense of obligation in freedom, that responsibility in fellowship, which is as far removed from all collectivism as it is from all individualism. What we need is first and foremost this understanding of things which would set us free from a false ecclesiasticism for the purpose of communion with our brethren. We need thus a real *communio sanctorum*: it is the only answer to communism falsely so-called.

Chapter Twelve

We started from the miracle of the *Ecclesia*, of the Christian fellowship, and we return to it. The Christian community is the great miracle of history, and history is the proof that the gates of hell shall not prevail against it. There can hardly be a more overwhelming personal experience of this miracle than when it is granted to one to greet brothers in Christ in the far east and the far west and in many lands inhabited by men of other races, tongues, and cultures, and to strengthen one's faith by uniting with them in common prayer to the one Lord. The institutions which we call churches, through a historical process lasting nearly 2,000 years, have built up the shell in which this precious kernel has been contained and preserved. It is certain that without these churches most of what we now rejoice in as the action and influence of the Christian mission would never have happened. In drawing attention to the fact that they have formed not merely a protective but also a concealing framework, we should not overlook the other fact, that they have proved instruments by whose help the Lord of the *Ecclesia* has both preserved and refashioned it ever afresh. In spite of everything, the institutional church has shown itself to be the most powerful *externum subsidium* of the Christian communion, from the days when the struggle with the heresies and fanaticisms of gnosis caused the *Ecclesia* to establish its monarchical episcopate and its quasi-political structure even to our times when in its fight against the totalitarian state of Hitler the dynamic Christian communion experienced once more the protection and stability which the official Church was able to offer it. Therefore it can never be a question of deriving from this distinction between the *Ecclesia* and the Church a merely negative judgment upon or a

116

hostile attitude towards the latter. A means which the providence of God has used for so long and to such powerful effect, must not be allowed to fall a victim to destructive criticism.

But this positive relation between *Ecclesia* and Church must not obscure for us the other fact that the Church has again and again stood revealed as one of the major obstacles to the creation and preservation of the true *Ecclesia*, and particularly so, when it has boasted of being identical with the Christian community and has named Christ and the Church in one breath. Not the hostility of the unbelieving world, but clerical parsonic ecclesiasticism has ever been the greatest enemy of the Christian message and of brotherhood rooted in Christ. *Ecrasez l'infame* is not only the cry of hatred uttered by the rationalistic enlightenment, it is also the cry of humanity oppressed by the Church and therefore the warning sign— never to be ignored—given by Christ Himself to a Christianity which is betraying Him in the interests of the Church.

The Church is a historically evolved form, a vessel of the *Ecclesia*; not to it, but to the *Ecclesia* alone, was given the promise of invincibility and eternal durability. Since Christianity for the first time in the Reformation era grasped the fact that the essence of the *Ecclesia* was in principle distinguishable from, and in part opposed to, the vessel of the church which contained it, ever new attempts have been made to give the Christian community the external form which best fits it. One of the most important results of the ecumenical movement has been to make Christianity aware of the multiplicity of these outward forms, and the necessity of their manifold variety. We have become painfully aware that the multiplicity of the churches calls in question the fundamental oneness of the *Ecclesia*: but whether this fundamental unity of the Christ-community requires unified expression in one church is extremely doubtful. Through ecumenical conversations we have learnt to realize the relative justification of all these various forms and the specific service which each of them in virtue of its special characteristics renders towards the maintenance, the purification, the strengthening and the propagation of the *Ecclesia*. In most recent times we have been compelled to recognize that the same *providentia Dei* which permitted the growth of the Church or churches, has brought into being totally new forms of Christian communion wherein any hint at the classic traditional ecclesiastical form has been consciously avoided. We must therefore be prepared for the possibility that it might be the will of God eventually to destroy the ancient churchly framework of the *Ecclesia* or at least—as is now already happening—to complete it by structures of a very different order. One of the chief practical concerns of this book has been to try to ensure that we do not oppose the divine intention by any self-willed *a priori* ecclesiasticism.

The second is this. During the whole course of its history, by reason of the fact that it was essentially a collective rather than a fellowship, the Church has not only neglected to create a true brotherhood in Christ, but in many ways has positively hindered such a development. Yet just here lies the essence of the New Testament *Ecclesia*—the oneness of communion with Christ by faith and brotherhood in love. Therefore efforts to create new forms of Christian communion at the present time are directed to this end and will be so much more in the future. It is because the Church has neglected in almost all ages to create a true fellowship in Christ that we are confronted by the phenomenon of modern communism which has grown like a wasting disease. With or without the churches, if necessary even in opposition to them, God will cause the *Ecclesia* to become a real community of brothers. Whether the churches yield to this recognition or on the contrary blind themselves to it will determine the question whether or not they have a future.

NOTES

CHAPTER ONE

(1) Calvin, *Institutio* IV. 1, 1; 1, 4.

(2) Calvin, *Institutio* 1, 4.

(3) Calvin, *Institutio* 1, 1; 1, 5. Craig, "The Church, her nature and task" (in *The Universal Church in God's Design*).

(4) Thornton, *The Common Life in the Body of Christ*.

(5) K. L. Schmidt in *Theol. Wörterbuch zum Neuen Testament* III, 515. Therefore it is questionable whether one may say, "it would be an epigrammatic exaggeration to assert that a single individual might and must be the *Ecclesia* if he has communion with Christ". As an exaggeration of the verticality of Christ, this is correct in contrast with any attempt to explain the *Ecclesia* sociologically. But the decisive factor in the *Ecclesia* is just that the vertical character of Christology and the horizontal character of human fellowship are inseparable. Bonhoeffer is therefore right when he says that communion with Christ can only be found in the *Ecclesia* (*Sanctorum Communio*, p. 88). Thornton demonstrates this most impressively and with rich Biblical quotations as far as the New Testament *koinonia* is concerned; *loc. cit.*

(6) According to the formula of the Roman Catholic church (Denzinger, *Enchiridion Symbolorum*, No. 1792).

(7) Luther WA, L, p. 625.

(8) WA, XXX. I, p. 189f.

(9) The many equivalents for *Ecclesia* in the New Testament in Schmidt, *op. cit.*, p. 520.

(10) The Swiss *Lexikon* says with regard to this (Vol. IV. 445), "The Institution is the most important form of the ordering of society. In the Institution is voiced the resolve to establish an order, as a result of which the relationships between men and concrete or ideal things are regulated: when it is fixed in writing, law is its highest form."

(11) Typical in this connection is the public utterance of a Zürich theologian: "The people of Zürich love their Church." This pronouncement is as true as it is also the expression of the widespread fundamental misunderstanding of the *Ecclesia*.

(12) The equation Church=*universitas christianorum* (which is a matter of course) is recognized naturally in Catholic circles too, says Loofs (*Symbolism*, p. 217) and then continues "The formulae of Augustine's spiritual conception of the Church live on, in part, therefore in modern catholicism". But it is characteristic that the self-interpretation of the Roman church is determined by the institution, by the papacy. One

cannot be a Christian and a member of the Church without believing in the Pope, according to the sense of the Vatican.

(13) As far as I am aware, Augustine does not yet use the phrase *ecclesia invisibilis*, but he certainly does distinguish between the *corpus verum* and the *corpus permixtum* and speaks of the *"numerus ille justorum qui secundum propositum coacti sunt"* and calls this a *"hortus conclusus"*. That means therefore that he has the idea but not the actual word *Ecclesia invisibilis*. But that this idea is decisive for Calvin's understanding of the Church, the first paragraphs of IV. 1 show already.

CHAPTER TWO

(1) So rightly E. F. Scott, *The Nature of the Early Church*, where it is stressed that it was of some importance to the early Christians to gain recognition as a sect; p. 30f. When Flew objects to this—"A sect is a party or school within Israel . . . but the disciples were Israel", he is right, only this appreciation is proper to a later stage of early Christianity, when the separation had already taken place (*Jesus and His Church*, p. 101).

(2) The passages in Calvin and Irenaeus I have cited in *Revelation and Reason*, p. 196.

(3) This conception corresponds exactly—if I understand aright—to that of Störm to which R. Nelson in his survey *The Realm of Redemption* refers. He characterizes the disciples prior to Good Friday and Easter as *"Ecclesia designata"* corresponding to the Messiah *"designatus"*. The discussion concerning the genuineness of Matt. 16:18 (and Matt. 18:15–18), the only passages where the word *Ecclesia* is found on the lips of Jesus, is a highly complicated matter both as regards the number of investigators taking part and the diversity of their views (see the summary in Linton, *The Problem of the Primitive Church*, p. 157ff. and the most recent comprehensive treatment in Kümmel's *Kirchenbegriff und Geschichtsbewusstsein in der Urgemeinde und bei Jesus*, 1943). In spite of the fact that to-day there is a tendency to affirm the genuineness of the passage in question, and very keen critics advocate this view, I must content myself with a *non liquet*. On the other hand a considerable consensus of opinion supports the statement of Edwin Lewis "that there was in any profound sense no Church until Christ had finished His work of conquering sin and death". (*The Ministry and the Sacraments*, p. 478.) The Christian fellowship in the strictly New Testament sense of *Ecclesia* (not "Church"!) does not begin until Easter and becomes definitely outlined only at Pentecost. On the other hand many serious critics agree with the above-mentioned idea that the Messiah Jesus already in His earthly life formed the nucleus of a Messianic people. So Dobschutz (ZNW 1929), Cullmann, *Die Königsbotschaft Christi*, Fridrichsen, *Eglise et sacrement dans le Nouveau Testament*.

Similarly Flew, *Jesus and His Church*. But I would take exception to the expression of Craig that Jesus "redeemed the already existing Church" (*The Universal Church in God's Design*, p. 33).

(4) Cf. Kattenbusch, *"der Quellort der Kirchenidee"*, in *Festgabe für Harnack*, p. 169ff.

CHAPTER THREE

(1) This aspect of the apostolate, which is the all-important one, is rather neglected by Sohm and all those who stress the pneumatic-charismatic factor. Not the apostolic *charisma*, but the historically contingent fact of revelation, eyewitnessing or witnessing in the most primary sense, constitutes the apostolate. Of course the exegetic-historical problem here is complicated by the fact that both in the New Testament and also later there are apostles who are not included among the primary witnesses. The discovery of the *Didache* by Bryennios, 1883, in which such apostles are represented as the authoritative leaders of the church, has no doubt been overstressed not only by Harnack but also by later critics: in any event it is this which gave rise to the charismatic conception of the apostolate. On the other hand it will not do, of course, to dismiss the *didache* as an insignificant apocryphon as do Gregory Dix and his Anglo-Catholic friends for obvious reasons (cf. *The Apostolic Ministry*, p. 240).

(2) Cf. I Cor. 2:10-15. It is hardly possible to conceive a stronger witness than this for the autonomy of the community grounded in the possession of the Holy Ghost. Here Paul expressly ranges himself with those possessed of spiritual gifts.

(3) I owe this recognition to the essay of E. Schweizer, *Gemeinde nach dem Neuen Testament* (Theological Studies published by Karl Barth, No. 26)—apart from the essay of Holl (see following note).

(4) Karl Holl, *Gesammelte Werke*, II, pp. 44-67.

(5) Cf. Schweizer, *op. cit.*

(6) Apart from Roman Catholics, this idea has been put forward very impressively by Anglo-Catholic theologians who published the composite volume *The Apostolic Ministry* (1949) and to whose circle belong, besides the Bishop of Oxford, Kirk, so distinguished a thinker as A. M. Farrer, so learned a patristic scholar as Gregory Dix and other capable scholars. Here we see at work those ideas which as driving forces motivated the (first) Oxford Movement in England. Unfortunately these have been very little known on the European continent. It is to be hoped that the somewhat important essays of this book will be taken more seriously and better heeded by our theologians than were those of its predecessor—the volume of essays published by Bishop Gore, *The Church and the Ministry*, new edition 1936. It would be decidedly useful for the understanding of the New Testament and the problem of the Church if Protestant theology

became acquainted with the Catholic view of the Church not merely in the framework of Roman Catholicism.

(7) The Biblical foundation of this conception in the *shaliach* theory, which G. Dix cites, is not new: before him already the Jew Vogelstein gave expression to it in an interesting way in his books *Die Entstehung und Entwicklung des Apostelates im Judentum* (1905) and *The Development of the Apostolate in Judaism and its Transformation in Christianity*, 1925.

(8) The way in which Farrer (*op. cit.*) translates the New Testament *diakonein*=serve, by a technical term of his own coining "to deacon", which relates to ecclesiastical offices, really turns things upside down.

In this connection it should be noted that for the ministries of which Paul speaks in 1 Cor. 12, the New Testament just does not use the ecclesiastical term *leiturgia* which might have been expected in view of the LXX, but uses on the contrary the absolutely lay, non-technical term *diakonia* and *diakonein* which means straightforward brotherly helpfulness as well as the service of the apostles. See on the other hand the details in T. W. Manson, *The Church's Ministry*, p. 26ff.

(9) This thought is well expressed by Jenkins, *The Nature of Catholicity*, p. 24 and by Newbigin, *The Reunion of the Church*, p. 164: that the Anglo-Catholic view is not that of the Anglican church as a whole is proved by the composite volume *The Ministry of the Church*.

CHAPTER FOUR

(1) One need only think of the fifteenth-century Popes accusing each other of heresy, or, in order to give a more modern example, of the fact that among the Anglican bishops presumably standing in apostolic succession, again and again black sheep are to be found whose rationalism is—justifiably—a thorn in the flesh to their orthodox colleagues.

(2) Cf. Rademacher, *Der Entwicklungsgedanke in Religion und Dogma*, *Rüstzeug der Gegenwart*, published by J. Frohberger, 1914; Alois Schmitt, *Katholizismus und Entwicklungsgedanke*, *Kath. Lebensworte*, 9th vol.; H. Ording, *Untersuchungen über Entwicklungslehre und Theologie*. All these are Roman Catholic writings. Quite similar thoughts are reflected in Anglo-Catholic views: one must never forget that the Anglo-Catholicism of the Newman-Pusey epoch is a child of romanticism.

(3) This sharp distinction between early and neo-catholicism is the exclusive merit of the great evangelical jurist Rudolph Sohm: unfortunately it is too little known to theologians since it is to be found in the posthumous and unfinished second volume of his Canon Law. The following citations are all taken from this work, *Canon Law*, Vol. 2, Catholic Canon Law.

(4) *op. cit.*, p. 78.

(5) *op. cit.*, p. 79.
(6) *op. cit.*, p. 83.
(7) *op. cit.*, p. 88.
(8) *op. cit.*, p. 103.
(9) *op. cit.*, p. 105.
(10) *op. cit.*, p. 107.
(11) *op. cit.*, p. 110.
(12) Loofs, *Symbolism*, p. 209.
(13) *Conc. Vaticanum* No. 1839.
(14) Sohm, *op. cit.*, p. 117. "The principle of tradition has been superseded by the development of an infallible administrative teaching office."
(15) An illuminating example of this tradition which is no tradition, but is theologically construed as such and dogmatically *credendum proponitur*, is all the dogmas concerning the Virgin Mary, especially the most recent regarding her bodily assumption. The Benedictine father Benedict Bauer writes: "Precisely this most glorious assumption of the Virgin Mary is veiled in the secrecy of silence. Scripture knows nothing of it." (*Petitiones de Assumptione Corporea B. V. Mariae* II, p. 422, Rome, Vatican City, 1942): not only that, but—"History has been silent for more than 500 years." F. Blanke rightly says and to him I owe this reference: "Catholic theologians are therefore convinced that the bodily assumption of Mary was a historical fact, but they teach that no man ever saw this happening" (*Die leibliche Himmelfahrt der Jungfrau Maria*, Zürich, 1950).

CHAPTER FIVE

(1) "According to this it is clear what the apostolic era thought of under the term Spirit: The supernatural power of God which produces marvels among men", Gunkel, *Die Wirkungen des heiligen Geistes*, p. 25. Similarly Weinel sums up: "The power exceeding that of men, mysterious in its nature and pointing to a higher source." (*Die Wirkungen des Geistes und der Geister.*)

(2) It is the apostle Paul who fused with his Christo-centric theology the still partially impersonal dynamism of the early period as reflected for example in the first chapters of the Acts, and so on the one hand related spirit and the knowledge of God (1 Cor. 2) and, on the other, derived from the same source the manifold variety of spiritual operations and gifts of grace (*charismata*) without allowing the one to prejudice the other.

(3) It seems to me that recently people have been talking at cross purposes about the question whether the Body of Christ is meant as a metaphor or literally. Doubtless something literally true is meant there-

by, as Thornton emphasizes (*The Common Life in the Body of Christ*, p. 256): but equally certainly this real Body of Christ is not a physical organism, rather this reality is compared with a physical organism (Eph. 4:12f.). E. Schweizer is of the same opinion in *The Life of the Lord in the Community and its Ministries*, p. 51. When Rawlinson in *Mysterium Christi* speaks of being literally incorporated in the Body of Christ, that doubtless corresponds to the New Testament idea of baptism (see above p. 80f.) but does not therefore cease to be a figurative expression, because this Body is not composed of physical members but of persons called members.

(4) That is the misunderstanding to which Sohm was always exposed —he who has done more than anyone for the understanding of this pneumatic-charismatic order of the *Ecclesia* in the first volume of his *Canon Law*. In this matter I agree with H. von Camperhausen, *Recht und Gehorsam in der ältesten Kirche* and with Kümmel's particulars in *Theol. Rundschau* V. 17, Pt. 1, p. 47; only, since now order and formal law have become identified, I would avoid the term "law" for this polity. Because matters stand thus, the main thesis of Sohm is valid.

(5) Bonhoeffer, *Nachfolge*, p. 160, disputes this distinction because he is considering only the theological confessional unity with the early church and forgetting the decisive factor of the dynamism of the Holy Ghost. I would say that the longing and petition for the pentecostal Spirit which speaks to us so impressively in the writings of the two Blumhardts, father and son, carries all the more weight in that they had experienced in Mottlingen and Bad Boll more of this dynamic power than the rest of the church in their day. To be conscious of this our lack of spiritual power is by no means to idealize the real *Ecclesia* of the New Testament. See above, pp. 95ff.

CHAPTER SIX

(1) Since the powerfully original work of Albert Schweitzer, *The Mysticism of the Apostle Paul*, this insight into the mystical character of the *Ecclesia* has been generally accepted. Unfortunately, Schweitzer did not recognize the unity of Paul's doctrine of justification with his Christ-mysticism; the decisive passage, Gal. 2:20, 21, which furnishes the classical testimony to this unity, does not appear, so far as I know, in Schweitzer's book. Therefore, since he does not realize the oneness of faith and so-called mysticism, he must describe the latter as naturalistic, p. 214ff. (and elsewhere) and the doctrine of justification is removed from its Pauline centrality to a peripheral polemical position. But apart from this, things of fundamental importance for the understanding of the *Ecclesia* may be learnt from Schweitzer's book.

(2) The passage already quoted in Galatians (2:20ff.) shows also how

wrong it is when Schweitzer affirms that only death, not the atoning death of Jesus, is the presupposition for the Christ-mysticism of Paul (*op. cit.*, p. 216ff.).

(3) With Schweitzer it is called not magical but naturalistic, because he does not recognize the unity of the cross and of being crucified with Christ—a unity which, as is well known, does not appear first in the Epistle to the Romans, but already in that to the Galatians (2:19, 6:14).

(4) This description of the state of the *Ecclesia*—now a theological commonplace—comes from Dodd; the insight thus expressed has become to-day almost common ground in New Testament scholarship but Dodd's reaction against purely futurist eschatology (i.e. thorough-going eschatology) has overshot the mark in so far as he pays too little regard to the element of expectation as opposed to that of secure possession of the (full) Messianic salvation. See following notes.

(5) Cf. Kümmel, *Verheissung und Erfüllung*.

(6) This is finely shown in the already mentioned work of Ed. Schweizer, where it is also pointed out that the differing emphasis of the "but already" and the "not yet" involves a differing attitude towards churchly authority—a divergence, however, which never hardens into a real contrast just because everywhere alongside the "but already" the "not yet" is recognized.

(7) This again is one of the insights which essentially we owe to A. Schweitzer, *The Mysticism of the Apostle Paul*, p. 164ff.

CHAPTER SEVEN

(1) So Karl Barth, "The Church, the living community of the living Lord Jesus Christ" (in: *Die Kirche in Gottes Heilsplan*).

(2) It is of the greatest significance that Paul in speaking of the practical everyday life of each individual Christian (Rom. 12:1f.) uses the cultic words "sacrifice" and "service of God" (*latreia*) while avoiding the latter when it is a question of cultic divine worship.

(3) Cullmann, *Urchristentum und Gottesdienst*, p. 23f.

(4) Cullmann, *op. cit.*, p. 24ff.

(5) The view cogently expressed by Cullmann that every religious service—apart from baptism—was *eo ipso* also a sacramental celebration, is not accepted by many scholars who rightly emphasize that in all probability unbelievers—of whom it is spoken in 1 Cor. 14—were not allowed to participate in the latter: the sacrament was, in this sense, from the very beginning, esoterical.

(6) A further expression of the paradoxical unity of the exclusively sacral and the familiar everyday element is to be seen in the fact that in the very earliest period the meal was obviously celebrated not only on

Sundays but also daily, and not merely at one central place but here and there in various houses. It was naturally linked up with the Habura—the daily meal—which Jesus was accustomed to celebrate with His disciples; this is still plain in Luke 24.

(7) So especially Cullmann, *op. cit.*, p. 31.

(8) The question whether John by narrating the footwashing scene wished to show his lack of interest in the Eucharist (Bultmann) or whether on the contrary the Fourth Gospel has an outright sacramentalist structure and is dominated by a sacramentalist philosophy, we can leave undecided.

(9) Cullmann, *op. cit.*, p. 31, emphasizes to such an extent the high significance of the Eucharist for the upbuilding of the community, that he almost loses sight of the other fact that the *Ecclesia* is a Christian fellowship and the Body of Christ even where there is no celebration but where two or three are gathered together; that therefore the Body of Christ is spoken of in the New Testament quite without any necessary reference to the Eucharist, and that the rarity of direct reference precludes an essentially sacramental understanding of the *Ecclesia*.

(10) The discussion about baptism has recently become very lively and has led to much controversy. Apart from the well-known works of Karl Barth, *The Doctrine of the Church regarding Baptism*, Cullmann, *Baptism in the New Testament*, I would mention also H. Grossman, *Ein Ja zur Kindertaufe*, Leenhardt, *Le Baptême Chrétien*, P. C. Marcel, *Le Baptême, Sacrement de l'Alliance de Grâce*, which last work is distinguished from the rest by a certain reformed-scholastic thoroughness and an absence of the critical-historical point of view. The causative character of baptism (Schlier, Leenhardt, Cullmann, Kümmel) as opposed to the purely cognitive (Barth) might stand; but it would be impossible to find with Schlier an *opus operatum* and salvation as a necessary effect of baptism in the New Testament (for the Church doctrine of baptism, *Th. Lit. Zeitg.*, 1947, pp. 321–336). In the Acts of the Apostles the view appears, as is known, that a person might receive the Holy Ghost without being baptized (Acts 10:44). Such passages make at least one thing clear—that there is no *necessary* connection between receiving the Holy Ghost and being baptized.

(11) Cf. esp. Marcel, *op. cit.*, pp. 145ff.

(12) The distinction established by Cullmann (*Baptism in the New Testament*) between faith before and faith after baptism corresponds to what we show in Chapter V about the para-logical manifestations of the Holy Ghost for the spread of the *Ecclesia*.

(13) That Zwingli's symbolic interpretation of the Last Supper which Jesus had with His disciples is exegetically correct, even the Lutheran L. von Loewenich must grant (*Vom Abendmahl*, p. 23ff.) although for the rest he rightly expresses belief in the real presence of Christ as both Luther and Calvin had done.

(14) So also Cullman: *Urchristentum und Gottesdienst,* p. 31.

(15) Here Cullman may well be right, *op. cit.,* p. 27, even if his thesis concerning the oneness of the primitive Christian divine service be rejected.

(16) Both continental and English scholars have independently stressed the relationship of early Christian baptism to the baptism of Jesus—Jeremias, Cullmann, Leenhardt, as also Flemington, *The New Testament Doctrine of Baptism.* At least since Matthew the relationship of the baptism of Jesus to the vicarious bearing of sin was an accepted notion in the *Ecclesia*; John 1:29ff. is only the crown and climax of a long development of this insight.

(17) The extremely rare references to the Eucharist in the New Testament and the way in which Paul (1 Cor. 1:14ff.) speaks of his own baptism forbids any sacramental over-valuation of baptism and Lord's Supper. Certainly in both cases the theme is central—the crucified and risen Lord of the community, the Head of the Body; but no one reading the New Testament without a knowledge of later Church history would suppose that the sacraments were the essential feature of the Christian community.

CHAPTER EIGHT

(1) From this it is clear how dubious is the method of (Anglo) Catholics who fill up the gaps in our knowledge of the apostolic age by conclusions drawn from later history. That is explicitly the case with G. Dix (*op. cit.,* p. 191).

(2) Albert Schweitzer (*The Mysticism of the Apostle Paul,* p. 264ff.) has very well noted the effect of this modification, the dawning interest in the elements of bread and wine as such; unfortunately his conception of Pauline mysticism as naturalistic misleads him into assuming an unjustified opposition between the Johannine and the Pauline ideas of salvation and causes him to read the Fourth Gospel in the light of Ignatius of Antioch. How great is the distance between Ignatius and the Johannine Gospel has recently been shown by Chr. Maurer, 1949 (*Ignatius von Antiochien und das Johannesevangelium*).

(3) Rud. Sohm's thesis (*Kirchenrecht,* I, § 13) that in the age of primitive Christianity the *Ecclesia* is one and that the *Ecclesiai* of Corinth and Thessalonica are only manifestations of the Christian community as a whole, is unanswerable, for it alone corresponds to the idea of the Body of Christ (quite in this sense, K. L. Schmidt, *op. cit.,* p. 508). Therefore when Paul speaks of the order of the *Ecclesia* he is thinking not of the local congregations but of the *Ecclesia* as a whole (1 Cor. 12:27ff.) and specifies as ministries of the *Ecclesia* only such as have a bearing on the Church as a whole—apostles, prophets, and teachers.

In the Jerusalem church there were gatherings for the sacramental meal in houses, *kat'oikon* (Acts 2:46). Of course 1 Cor. 11-20 assumes that the Corinthian Christians congregate in one place; but not until the first epistle of Clement is the principle formulated that only in one place may the meal be celebrated (1 Cl. 40, 41) because the Jewish sacrifices might be performed only in the temple. We see here already therefore the comparison of the Eucharist with the Old Testament sacrifice. Moreover it makes little difference whether one regards the monarchical priestly bishop as a cause or an effect of the concentration of the local community; there is a reciprocal influence exerted by the tendency towards the episcopal institution and that towards sacramentalism. From all this it is clear that the principle of congregationalism, according to which the Church is envisaged as the totality of individual congregations, does not correspond to the New Testament *Ecclesia*; the apostolic age simply does not know any such thing as an individual congregation. The *Ecclesia* in Corinth is not *an* Ecclesia but a manifestation of *the* Ecclesia.

(4) This inherently probable exchange of influences between eucharistic sacramentalism, monarchical episcopate and the requirement that the local community should be one is plainly to be seen in Ignatius.

(5) The mutual conditioning of sacramentalism and institutionalism was not properly realized by Sohm. In spite of that, to no other besides this Christian jurist do we owe so much in regard to the understanding of the *Ecclesia*. His great contribution is to have recognized the early penetration of canon law, of institutionalism. The heresy of Harnack (Farrer, *Apostolic Ministry*, p. 145) consists according to Farrer precisely in what Sohm was the first to recognize correctly, but Sohm takes over from Harnack the well-grounded idea that in the earliest period the *episkopoi* were the officials whose duty it was to offer thanksgiving for the eucharistic gifts of the congregation and to administer the property of the Church. But quite rightly he does not allow the supposition that they were therefore merely administrative, not spiritual officers. Even the administration of church property is a spiritual matter in the apostolic community; it takes place by the command of God, through a teaching officer (Sohm, *op. cit.*, p. 84). The offering of thanks and distribution of alms is a thoroughly spiritual task. The transference of teaching duties to the bishop in the pastoral epistles is therefore not a complete innovation. The new departure, however, is plainly revealed in the letter of Ignatius where the bishop, because he administers the Eucharist as the food of salvation, confronts the laity as a priest and as the vicar of Christ.

(6) Should the views of Chr. Eggenberger (*Die Quellen der politischen Ethik des 1 Klemensbriefes*, Zürich, 1951) be accepted—that the first epistle of Clement is a pseudonymous document dependent upon Dion von Prusa, the extoller of the Roman empire, and therefore not that known to Irenaeus, this would not lessen the importance of the letter as a stage in the ecclesiastical transformation of the *Ecclesia*, but a non-Christian

source of this change and, as such, a characteristically political heathen Roman view would thereby have been discovered.

(7) The bishops' lists of Hegesippus mentioned by Eusebius, on which especially the doctrine of apostolic succession is based, do not of course reach back with certainty to the apostolic age, as even the Anglo-Catholic G. Dix admits (*The Apostolic Ministry*, p. 208); but there can be no doubt certain congregations long remembered that their leaders had once been instituted by apostles; the pastoral epistles are to be valued as symptomatic of this growing interest in the apostolic succession.

(8) Cf. the beautiful ordination prayer in the Church Order of Hippolytus (*Neutestamentliche Apokryphen*, pub. Hennecke, p. 574f.). In this writing *cheirotonia* appears already to mean as much as ordination by laying on of hands.

CHAPTER NINE

(1) The primitive church was of course aware that the fundamental testimonies collected in the Canon were only in part writings of the apostles; it also recognized as canonical-apostolic testimony writings by disciples of the apostles such as the gospels of Mark and Luke and the Acts. The norm of primary testimony is not thereby impaired but rather interpreted generously (cf. Kümmel, *Notwendigkeit und Grenze des neutestamentlichen Kanons*, Zeit. f. Theol. und Kirche, 1950, pp. 277–312).

(2) "One must regard the bishop as the Lord Himself." Ignatius, Eph. 6, 2. "Subject to the bishop as the grace of God, to the presbytery as the law of Jesus Christ" (Magn. 3, 1). "Be subject to the bishop as to Jesus Christ" (Trall. 2, 1), "inseparable from God, Jesus Christ and the bishop". With Ignatius it is plain beyond all doubt that the bishop has this high significance as the man of the altar, of the temple and altar precincts (for example Trall. 6, 2; Phil. 4) "one altar, one bishop": only that Eucharist is valid which is celebrated under the bishop's authority (Smyrn. 8, 1). "Whosoever honours the bishop, is honoured of God, whosoever does anything without the bishop, serves the devil" (9, 1). "Hold fast to the bishop, so that God may hold fast to you" (Pol. 6, 1).

Even when we can understand that in the storms and struggles of those times, the unity and stability which a bishop could offer the community were of great importance, it is staggering to see that already at the beginning of the second century the institution of the episcopate had been exalted to such godlike dignity. The power which thus exalted it was that of the altar and the sacrament.

(3) We may interpret the incidents in Corinth to which Clement of Rome refers in his epistle, as such a revolt against the episcopal churchly transformation of the *Ecclesia*.

CHAPTER TEN

(1) So for example the Coptic Church of the Monophysites, dating from 563, or the Nestorian Church from 483, which became very important for the spread of Christianity in the Middle and Far East.

(2) E. Troeltsch styles the post-Reformation Free Churches of the West unhesitatingly as neo-Calvinistic (cf. *Social Teaching*, p. 733ff.).

(3) How Luther really understood the Church, i.e. what he thought of its working out in practice, is most clearly to be seen in his writing *Deutsche Messe und Ordnung des Gottesdienstes*, 1526 (WA, XIX, p. 72f.)—unfortunately still too little known. But he confesses "I can and may not yet set up and organize such a community or congregation. For I have not yet the people that would be required" (p. 75).

(4) Cf. K. Holl, *Luther und das landesherrliche Kirchenregiment* (*Ges. Werke*, I, pp. 326–389). Unfortunately Holl's conception of Luther's Church outlook is shaped by the idea of the invisible Church which is Augustinian in provenance, Zwinglian and Calvinistic, but foreign to Luther himself (cf. *Die Entstehung von Luthers Kirchenbegriff*, *loc. cit.*, pp. 288–306). The best that has so far been written about Luther's idea of the Church is in my opinion the small and little known work of Ernst Rietschel—*Das Problem der unsichtbaren Kirche bei Luther*, 1932.

(5) Luther's conception of the ministry is certainly complex. As an organized institution, it is of this world; but as a commission given to the community by Christ for the preaching of the Gospel, it is of course spiritual. Again it is spiritually irrelevant how and to whom the community entrusts this office, so long as it is to a member of the community. The latter must, however, be careful to see that the appointed minister really preaches the Word of God and not foreign doctrine.

(6) Newman's *Apologia Pro Vita Sua* is extremely informative as regards the driving force behind the Anglo-Catholic reform movement; what Newman relates concerning his earliest co-worker and inspirer Froude, "he was powerfully drawn to the mediaeval church, but not to the primitive" (p. 47) and "he made me look with admiration towards the church of Rome and in the same degree to dislike the Reformation" (p. 48) is so much the more remarkable that it concerns the time before the actual beginning of the Anglo-Catholic movement proper. The New Testament (the primitive church) was not—and is still not—the norm and real point of orientation for Anglo-Catholic thought.

(7) In so far as the catholic churches acknowledge this finality of Scripture as a norm, real conversation with them is still always a possibility. The Roman church has automatically excluded itself from such conversation by the dogma that the Pope is the sole authoritative exponent of Scripture; it has made ineffectual both Scripture and tradition as a critical norm.

(8) The notion *"vera ecclesia"* was introduced by Melanchthon. (Cf. Otto Ritschl, *Dogmengeshichte des Protestantismus I*, p. 311ff., who seems to me to have grasped more clearly than Seeberg (*Dogmengeschichte*, V, p. 450f.) the turning point which Melanchthon occasioned in the Lutheran ecclesiastical outlook; though it is to the credit of Seeberg that he is able to give some Luther quotations). What Luther was concerned about and what Melanchthon was concerned about were two fundamentally different things. Melanchthon is the author of the idea that the true Church is empirically shown to be such by its teaching of pure orthodox doctrine.

(9) Any one who has once grasped the essential nature of the New Testament *Ecclesia* can only note with a certain humour the way in which Farrer at the conclusion of his essay on "The Ministry in the New Testament" (Additional note; St. Peter, p. 181f.) separates himself from Rome: "The apostles formed a college with Peter as president"; and again, concerning the Roman use of Matt. 16:18, "you cannot squeeze canon law out of poetry"—to which we can only add a hearty and ironical "indeed not"!

(10) Cf. Note 2 to IV *op. cit.*

(11) In emphasizing nowadays, and rightly so, that Calvin wished to form a church that should be independent of the state, and partly succeeded in doing so, it should not be overlooked that he, in common with his Scottish and later American English successors, continued to hold firm to the principle *cujus regio ejus religio*. John Milton and Roger Williams were the first to pave the way for the idea of tolerance; in point of fact, the latter is a product of the enlightenment and French Revolution.

CHAPTER ELEVEN

(1) A particularly impressive example of such a non-churchly *Ecclesia* movement became known to me in Japan. There exist there, called into being by the powerful personality of the first Japanese evangelist, Kanzo Utschimu:a, a whole series of groups mostly consisting of university professors and students, where the gospel is preached and divine service held in the simplest manner, which publish perhaps the best Biblical studies and quite a number of journals of native style, and which have no doubt done as much for the success of the Christian mission in Japan as have the official churches.

(2) In certain ecumenical circles we have often heard the phrase "rediscovery of the Church" as implying one of the greatest events of our time; I suppose that it is here a question not of the rediscovery of the New Testament *Ecclesia*, but of something quite different, namely, a revival of that false ecclesiasticism whose final goal—still unperceived at

present—can be no other than the Roman church. Equally dangerous do we consider the phrase often heard in the same circles and coming from theological quarters—"Let the Church be the Church!" This phrase had its real justification in the days of the German church's struggle against Hitler's programme of fusing the church with the Nazi state. But, hardened into a slogan and dissociated from that time of acute distress, it can become dangerously seductive, leading to a new clericalism and ecclesiasticism. *Caveant consules!* ecclesiasticism and clericalism are inextricably associated with the mere word "church"; therefore we are careful, when we are unable to avoid its use, to underline it twice!

Printed in the United States
134373LV00001B/22/A